Called to Be a Pastor

Called to Be a Pastor

Why It Matters to Both Congregations and Clergy

LARRY HAUDER
Foreword by Arthur Paul Boers

WIPF & STOCK · Eugene, Oregon

Called to Be a Pastor
Why It Matters to Both Congregations and Clergy

Wipf & Stock
An Imprint of Wipf and Stock Publishers
199 W. 8th Ave., Suite 3
Eugene, OR 97401

www.wipfandstock.com

ISBN 13: 978-1-4982-2125-2

Manufactured in the U.S.A.   07/06/2015

To Rebecca, my wife, best friend, and lifelong companion. To Nathan and Leah, forever and lovingly PKs.

Contents

Foreword

THERE IS WISDOM APLENTY here for any pastoral ministry setting. Larry Hauder's sagacious observations certainly apply as I reflect on my own pastoring—whether it was in the inner city, in a church planting, in a rural congregation, or in suburbia. Hauder's book is a rich tapestry of memoir, wise counsel, and practical advice. This is all rooted in Larry's ability to testify to what he has seen and practiced over the decades, both as a young man called to pastoring and later as a seasoned judicatory official and church consultant.

Larry testifies to how God was active in his life and in the congregations where he worked. More than that, he inspires us with down-to-earth reflections that demonstrate that God can be and is at work in our lives too.

This modest testimony is not about a grandstanding superstar who single-handedly launched massive enterprises and now bills himself as an "expert." Rather, as Larry makes sense of his own life and ministry, he invites us to take seriously our own ordinary lives and ministry possibilities. He is a receptive pilgrim inviting other pilgrims on a common path.

Larry Hauder's vision is appealing in two senses. For one, it is good to learn about and learn from a life and ministry lived well; that's certainly appealing. For another, seeing such a witness also appeals to us to walk in trust with God in our own opportunities for ministry.

Arthur Paul Boers

Acknowledgments

REBECCA, MY WIFE, WHOSE encouragement and tireless editing helped make possible *Called to Be a Pastor.* Likewise, Rebecca's commitment to co-labor with me in pastoral ministry is never forgotten.

Nathan and Leah, my children, whose influence made my worldview larger and my pastoral call more pliable

Hyde Park Mennonite Fellowship, where so many ministry opportunities were made available. This congregation provided me the space and encouragement to grow and mature as a pastor, for which I am grateful.

David Boshart, an exceptional conference executive who made all the difference when he said, "You need to get this manuscript published! I'll buy the first ten copies for new pastors in my conference."

Nancy Kauffmann, a trusted denominational executive who kept asking, "How are you coming on the book? You need to keep writing!"

Friends and peers who read all or parts of the manuscript, and encouraged me: Bobbie Birdsall, Jonathan Bryan, Robert Hartzler, Nancy Heisey, Michael King, Weldon Nisly, Robert Rainville, and Gary Sandusky.

Introduction

How DID I, A salt-and-pepper-haired pastor, arrive at this place—a holy place of unparalleled affection and respect for the local congregation? Yes, congregational ministry has given me great vocational satisfaction and a sense of life-purpose and joy. I cannot imagine feeling more fulfilled or spiritually alive had I declined the divine call to enter pastoral ministry. Yet, for others, this same vocation has caused much spiritual and emotional trauma, leaving pastors and their families confused and angry. And, I hasten to add, it's not only pastors and their families that get caught in the pain of pastoral ministry gone awry; the entire congregation experiences the tensions and spiritual fallout.

As much as one might want to chronicle the events leading up to a pastoral call, it eludes a neat recounting. There are simply too many contributing factors. The call originates incrementally and has some identifying markers, but it's also multi-generational, originating long before a nudging to consider the pastoral vocation or accepting a congregational invitation. Even after accepting an invitation, the call is an ongoing process—weekly, monthly, yearly—as pastors mature and grow into their identity and relate to a congregation.

From my perspective, a symbiotic relationship exists between pastors and the congregations they serve. Congregations hold the embryo of a pastoral call, much the same way as fertile earth holds the potential of a freshly planted seed. A pastor's call to preach and lead a congregation can either be nurtured to grow within the life of the local congregation, or it can shrivel and wilt. Neither can serve their function without the other's cooperation.

The more fully a pastoral candidate is able to grasp at least some of the complex dynamics of the pastor/congregation relationship, the better the chances for a successful pastorate. Likewise, congregations owe it to themselves and their pastor to better understand their role in the relationship: that of co-laboring with the pastor to accomplish God's purpose.

In *Called to Be a Pastor* I examine the circumstances that led to my life-altering decision to enter pastoral ministry. Just as importantly, I give consideration to the congregational dynamic that enabled my pastoral call to take root, grow, and become strong and secure. These insights seem vital to share with anyone considering pastoral ministry as well as with those in the pew. Pastors already in ministry will also find reference points that will stimulate personal reflections.

PURPOSE

Lay leaders, pastors, and individuals considering pastoral ministry will find encouragement and conversational resource material here. Congregations and pastors will discover ways to make their unique relationship more elastic, compassionate, and meaningful. But this plea for a more supple relationship should not be confused with the absence of clear expectations. Pastors and congregations do much better when their relationship is defined by clearly demarcated boundaries.

The Mennonite Church, my denominational home, along with other denominations, have historically had difficulty filling pastoral vacancies. The shortage of pastors seems to have lessened, at least for the time being, but a pair of significant questions still remains: Will those pastors find their role fulfilling? Will the congregations they serve prosper? My sense is that prospective candidates need a better understanding of how the pastor/congregation relationship works and what is needed in order to have a successful partnership in ministry.

Individuals considering service in the local church also require resources that help them think realistically about the position to which they aspire. In these pages, I hope they will find the encouragement to continue or the strength to re-examine their sense of call. Just as importantly, I hope that local congregational leaders will appreciate, in an outstanding way, the responsibility they have to encourage and mentor those considering pastoral ministry.

Small and medium-sized congregations, sometimes referred to as family or pastor-sized churches, will benefit most from reading *Called to Be a Pastor*. The centrality of the pastor's role is significant in these congregations because pastors are required to have expertise and central involvement in many ministry areas. Indeed, clergy is often at the center of congregational life. In churches where budgets and staff are limited, encouraging a high level of volunteerism is tremendously important. Thus, the primary pastoral task is to form effective partnerships with many volunteer lay leaders.

A REALITY CHECK

Few messages are more difficult to deliver than telling a pastor his support in the congregation has fallen below a healthy level, and he would be wise to consider resigning. During my near fifteen-year tenure as a conference minister to thirty-five congregations, I had the displeasure of overseeing the involuntary dismissal of far too many pastors. One particular conversation stands out as especially hard: "For the sake of your family and your own spiritual and mental health, I would suggest you resign from this pastorate. The amount of resistance to your leadership is quite strong. If, on the other hand, you choose to stay, I'll do the best I can to assist you and the congregation, including the retention of a consultant. The restoration process will most likely be long and stressful." I vividly remember delivering this message to a pastor and his spouse in their living room, with their three small children already asleep in the next room. Recalling this encounter still brings me goose bumps. Unfortunately, this pastor, as with most others who involuntarily resign, permanently left pastoral ministry.

I hasten to add that when the relationship between pastor and congregation is working well—as many do—there can be no higher vocational satisfaction. To witness a congregation in love with their pastor and a pastor that honors the congregation through faithful service is rewarding. In my ministry, I was fortunate enough to experience this kind of partnership.

METHOD

Stories can be powerful. Through sharing some of my own story and those of others, I hope to inspire my readers to consider their own spiritual journey with Christ and in the church. Everyone has a story to tell. This is not to say that theology and best practice theory is missing, but my intention is to help readers connect to the issues surrounding this amazing vocation. *Called to Be a Pastor* describes a personal journey through almost forty years of pastoral ministry. Nearly all of that experience was in a local congregation, and as a regional pastor responsible for congregational oversight as a judicatory. For the last several of years, I've served as a consultant to a variety of denominations.

I am a pastor, not a theologian; a practitioner, not a specialist. Therefore, any organizational polity, ministry theory, or theological discussions that arise out of reading this account will be a result of interacting with my story and relating it to personal experiences.

The reader will find a plethora of Scripture in each chapter. The Bible citations provide a foundation for the points I'm making. Scripture references also offer a window into my pastoral theology and how I use the Bible to think about ministry. Please also note that readers will find references to pastors of both genders. The use of "he" or "she" to describe pastors has been done arbitrarily, with no specific intention aside from sensitivity to the reality that there are both male and female pastors.

Each chapter begins with a "Journal Entry." These short excerpts were harvested from the volumes of daily entries in the many personal journals written throughout my ministry. These vignettes give a feel for my thoughts related to the chapter topics.

ASSUMPTIONS

I begin with certain assumptions, and the first is that the call to pastoral ministry is unique to each person. God has called people of faith into ministry since the beginning of recorded time, and my call is part of this historic, divine encounter. What is uniquely individualized in each pastoral call are the encompassing circumstances. Therefore, my story will be different from others, even though there will be overlap in purpose, theology, and chronology with other stories. If one expects a pastoral call to have a blinding light component like the Apostle Paul's, or a whale encounter like Jonah's, there will be disappointment. Not many pastors have those vivid call experiences, and neither did I.

A second assumption is that pastoral gifts can be of average grade. There was little evidence pointing toward special talents that would have predisposed me to be a good pastor. A productive and successful pastoral ministry is not about a certain personality type, high intellectual ability, or being a particularly gifted speaker, counselor, or administrator. What seems most important, from my perspective, is a solid sense of self and an identity that is emotionally and spiritually secure.

A third assumption is that congregations are as distinctly different as the pastors they call. Because each is unique, pastoral candidates will do a congregation and themselves a great favor by exploring a congregation's pastoral history and its missional trajectory. Likewise, congregational leaders will save themselves, and the congregations they serve, much pain and suffering by taking the necessary time to learn from the past and clarify their expectations for an incoming pastor.

A final assumption is that my tradition—Anabaptist Mennonite—is not unique in its challenges related to congregation and pastor relationships. These relationships are always delicate, regardless of the denomination, and the partnership is important to the spiritual health of both. Just as important as the bond between them, however, is the opportunity they have to advance the kingdom of God. This goal is realized best when the body of Christ is functioning at an optimum level, with the pastor and congregation working in tandem. Here is the overarching motivation for my decision to write *Called to Be a Pastor*.

1

A Life-Changing Invitation
—Called to Be a Pastor

In the year that King Uzziah died, I saw the Lord sitting on the throne,
high and lofty; and the hem of his robe filled the temple.

—Isa 6:1

Journal Entry

*I often hear people use phrases like, "God said" or "God told me."
Their language sounds so self-assured, like God speaks to them in
such personal and intimate ways. Their experience is vastly different from mine. God's Spirit does not speak to me as clearly. Then
again, maybe God does communicate to me just as plainly as the
next person, but I use a different language for giving testimony to
God's leading.*

DURING MY FIFTH YEAR as a public high school teacher, I felt the
first nudging, the first prodding, to consider becoming a pastor.

This vocational agitation came in the form of a seemingly innocent question from a fellow church member, "Larry, have you ever considered attending seminary?" This query, and my eventual decision to attend seminary, would forever change my life and that of my family. I would make the same decision today. There are a few regrets, but no serious second thoughts regarding my pastoral call and ministry vocation.

Looking back, I see more clearly how God's call took shape and actually led to my ordination certificate. But, at the time, God's invitation to consider pastoral ministry as an alternative to my high school teaching profession was evolutionary and often confusing. For example, I attended seminary with no clear vision of becoming a pastor. My stated purpose for enrolling was to work toward an advanced degree in education. Teaching remained my vocational priority, only the subject matter might be different in the future—at least, that was my assumption at the time. The decision to apply for a pastorate with a specific congregation would come a few years later, while I was enrolled in seminary.

Describing this pastoral call to others always proves complex, primarily because the narrative is long and lacking a climactic culmination. Most folks, myself included, want a rendition that delivers a punch line—a moment with an "aha" finale. Early in my call, I expected an important bright light experience similar to the Apostle Paul's or a glimpse into heaven as Isaiah had, but these historic, life-changing events belonged to them and were not mine to claim.

Well-meaning friends and acquaintances frequently asked, "When did you hear God speak to you about going into ministry?" The words of Jesus in John 10:39 gave me confidence that I did hear Christ's call and had followed as God's Spirit led me into pastoral ministry: "The Gatekeeper opens the gate for him, and the sheep hear his voice. He calls his own sheep by name and leads them out."

My pastoral call, though gradually unfolding, formed the foundation for an ongoing commitment to ministry. During times of congregational stress, or when my vocational identity seemed to lack potency, rehearsing my call narrative was vitally important. Remembering and retelling the stories that shaped this call, though often only to myself, provided encouragement and motivation to continue.

Looking back to the decision to attend seminary, I recall the difficulty of telling family and friends. Even though few, if any, of these friends or family had any familiarity with seminary or a pastoral call, they seemed to expect something different than what my lifestyle testimony demonstrated. Their image of a university created for the purpose of educating pastors and priests came loaded with many preconceptions, and I simply didn't fit the stereotype. Those closest to me knew me as someone other than a prime candidate for beginning graduate studies in theological education. Whatever that ideal student looked like, I didn't seem to fit the description. Teaching peers knew me as a dedicated fellow teacher, but not the guy they could imagine as a preacher. After all, I could tell a good joke, laugh at theirs, drink a beer with them on Friday after class, and join in on their conversations complaining about school administration policy.

Even high school friends raised a suspicious eyebrow when hearing about my seminary decision. High school was a time for socializing at the expense of study, and I ultimately departed for college on academic probation. Having a bachelor's degree in business education didn't inspire much holy confidence; neither did starting a wholesale Native American jewelry business when my wife and I lived in the Southwest. Adding to the list of unlikely traits for a Mennonite pastor candidate was a smoking habit developed in college. An outdoor kind of guy who enjoyed bird hunting with a black Lab and going off-road with a new Land Cruiser didn't really fit the image either. And only recently had my wife and I started attending church after a near eight-year hiatus. Yes, telling acquaintances about going to seminary caught most by surprise: "What are we missing here? You don't seem like the type!"

Beginning a conversation with my wife regarding a possible move gave me tremendous pause. The talk began something like this: "Honey, would you think I'm crazy to suggest we quit our jobs, leave our friends, and move halfway across the US so I can attend seminary?" Her response is hard to describe. Shock maybe says it best—something close to what I experienced years earlier when I told her my father had unexpectedly died. The thought of us leaving the Southwest for seminary was new, and it created much uncertainty—for her and for me.

A pastoral call needs to begin somewhere, and mine began with a question. At least, that's where I can clearly demarcate an inner awakening to the idea. Doreen, a saintly woman twenty years my senior and lay leader in the church, was the one who asked me the famous question: "Larry, have you ever considered attending seminary?" At the time of her question, becoming a pastor had never been something I had imagined for my future. The idea, simply put, had never registered on my "Richter scale." However, after enrolling in seminary, the transformation from imagining myself as a teacher of religion to a congregational pastor was not so immense.

There was a growing discontent in my current vocation, however, that made the question thought-provoking and potentially life-altering. (But doesn't God always use the common occurrences of life to get our attention?) A reoccurring thought kept pacing through my mind—that teaching high school was temporary. I ruminated on it like a cow chewing its cud. Even though I enjoyed working with high school kids, something was missing. Imagining a future in the classroom was no longer inspiring. Many of my teacher peers had lost excitement for their work as well. They lived for the 3:30 Friday afternoon dismissal bell. The school parking lot emptied quickly, and happy hour with fellow teachers became our way to salute another week survived. Is this what I wanted for the next thirty years? No, was my existential response.

In hindsight, I've wondered where my negative feelings about continuing a career in teaching came from. Why was I so convinced that teaching, for me, was a poor long-term vocational choice? The answers are not at all clear. I know many great teachers who have had lifelong, highly meaningful careers. Maybe I needed to experience a lack of fulfillment in one profession in order to be open to possibilities in another.

There were a number of other circumstances, apart from my restlessness with a teaching career, that also helped turn my head away from public school education and toward attending seminary. One major life transition was the birth of our first child. Parenthood was, by far, the biggest adjustment in our first five years of marriage. A first child seemed to be a catalyst for awakening my dormant faith. Suddenly, the spiritual care and wellbeing of a baby became a priority and a matter of significant deliberation between my wife and me. One result of these discussions was that we began attending church more regularly—a pattern I would see repeated with other new parents after I became a pastor.

Everyone needed to participate in the programs of this small congregation we joined. After all, the pastor was bi-vocational and had only limited time to give to pastoral ministry. Because he worked as a carpenter during the week and preached on Sunday, others were asked to lead worship, preach on occasion, and care for the needs of members. This faith community reminded me a lot of my home congregation, which was intimate and family-like. Sunday carry-in meals were common, as were invitations to other member's homes for a meal or social outing.

I quickly became involved in a variety of ministries: teaching the teenage Sunday school class, leading a building remodel committee, and eventually becoming the chairperson of the congregation. I experienced a sense of accomplishment and joy when volunteering in the church, quite different from my work in the public school classroom. During this time of intense congregational involvement was when Doreen asked the cathartic question, "Larry, have you ever thought about attending seminary?"

Soon thereafter, a well-known guest speaker provided a series of sermons for the congregation's "Missions Emphasis Week." The guest speaker's text was taken from Galatians: "the fruit of the Spirit is love, joy, peace, patience, kindness generosity, faithfulness, gentleness, and self-control" (Gal 5:22). The pastor's words led me to read the text in a way I hadn't before, making the messages more interesting and powerful than ever before.

We hosted Don, the visiting preacher, in our home. Our time with him provided my wife and I the opportunity to discuss matters of faith, belief, and the wider church. These conversations formed part of the foundation for the major life-changing decision to leave our home in the Southwest, attend seminary, and submit my name as a pastoral candidate a few years later.

Another life circumstance that lay dormant to any obvious conviction to pursue seminary was the death of my father a few years earlier. Being sudden and unexpected, his death was particularly traumatic. We had not been estranged, as fathers and sons sometimes are, but there were unfinished conversations between us. Although I saw no apparent connection between his death and my vocational decision at the time, as I look back, I see how this life-altering experience might have sowed the seedbed for my vocational unrest.

Clearly, a convergence of circumstances and family history enabled me to hear God open the door to a pastoral ministry career. Those life events included: vocational unrest, the birth of a first child, involvement in a local congregation, a visiting mission's speaker, a cooperative spouse, the death of a parent, and a wise church member taking a personal interest. This confluence made me amenable and receptive to that crucial "Larry, have you ever thought about attending seminary" question. I heard Doreen's query the way people of faith almost always hear calls—at an opportune moment in their lives. A few years later, a denominational mission executive, Ray, asked me, "Would you consider becoming a pastor to one of our many congregations out West that are in need?" Being near graduation, loving my classes, and talking over coffee with my fellow students—most of whom going into pastoral ministry—prepared me for Ray's question, just as life had prepared me for Doreen's.

A divine call usually makes the most sense to the person hearing the call, yet it's not necessarily understood or viewed as important by others. For instance, following graduation from the seminary, I returned to this intimate congregation, anxious to thank Doreen for encouraging me. When the appropriate opportunity presented, I said, "Doreen, do you remember asking me about attending seminary?" To my disappointment, she had no recollection! Her response, however, does beg the question: Because Doreen didn't remember asking me the famous question, is my interpretation invalidated? I don't think so.

God's intentions seem to be made clear only to those who can hear them: "Let anyone with ears to hear listen!" (Mark 4:9). But those intentions take time to understand, and it takes a community of friends and the church to assist in their translation.

There is no lack of dramatic calls by God in Scripture: Jonah's call to Nineveh (Jonah 1:1–3); the Apostle Paul's blinding light (Acts 9:3); Isaiah's glimpse into heaven (Isa 6:1–9); and Samuel's nighttime voices (Sam 3:1–10). These vivid experiences all seem newsworthy enough to capture the local headline news, yet each one is principally a personal experience understood chiefly by the main character involved. These accounts might be illustrative for teaching theology, but they are less helpful if one believes they should be imitated.

For example, I have found personal meaning in the call of Isaiah through a vision glimpsed while looking into heaven. The portrayal is majestic, complete with heavenly bodies and musical sounds. God allows Isaiah a glimpse into eternity, seemingly for the purpose of pursuing Isaiah. This cathartic, life-changing encounter with God sets a tone for Isaiah's future ministry. Isaiah's vision empowers him through troubling times, even when his prophetic role becomes discouraging, as evidenced in Isa 41:10.

Assuming that Isaiah's experience, complete with his life-altering vision, is also going to occur to me is problematic. My ministry call and divine encounter was different. The theology of a pastoral call is embedded in the knowledge that humans hear God in a variety of ways and places. None of the biblical experiences documenting encounters with God should be thought of as a model to duplicate.

Yet some people want to emulate the drama and excitement of Jonah, Isaiah, or the Apostle Paul. When I became a pastor, there were occasions when a congregant would speak with me about a pastoral ministry call. For example, a young family man came to my office and said he was going to quit his job as a butcher and attend a Bible school. There was a triumphal tone of an announcement rather than a spirit of humility in his words as he told his account of God's calling. His private language describing how "God has spoken to me" was perplexing. Instead of building credibility, his testimony became a reason for doubt. I was quite direct in suggesting he take more time in deliberation and prayer. Rather than listen, he packed up his family and moved them across the country to attend a Bible college. After a failed pastorate, he went back to his old profession. The unsuspecting congregation that called him paid a heavy price.

Contrast this story with another seeker, a car mechanic who immensely enjoyed his job as a congregational lay leader. He too wondered if this might be a sign to enter pastoral ministry. His spirit seemed pliable and genuine, and his family was supportive. Even though he lacked a college degree, Frank was continually reading. Following a three-year intensive correspondence course through a denominational distance-learning program, he entered a professional pastoral licensing program. His entire congregation rooted for his continued success. Frank went on to complete his studies and became a successful pastor in his home congregation.

After making the decision to attend seminary, I gave up my contract with the public schools, a significant decision since I had been granted tenure only a year earlier, which had been a long-pursued personal objective. Giving up this security and heading off to vocational uncertainty did, at times, feel foolish—like a child choosing to ignore a wise parent's advice. However, I also felt a certain whimsical freedom as a twenty-seven-year-old that today might look like bad decision-making. While the decision to attend seminary was made in full agreement with my spouse, I'm not sure I would counsel my children to do the same. Yet again, the call to pastoral ministry, not unlike other vocational ambitions, requires boldness seldom understood by others, which sometimes only makes sense to those who have felt called by God.

Two years after the pivotal seminary question was asked, my family and I moved from our beloved Southwest to Indiana. With a full U-Haul truck, Rebecca and I said goodbye to close friends and to the Hispanic, Native American culture we enjoyed so much. Our first child had been born there, and nesting had already begun.

My tear-filled eyes and wet cheeks are a lasting memory as I think about that truck rolling down Interstate 40 heading east. Struggling with her own sense of loss at saying goodbye to the familiar, Rebecca and our one-year-old son followed in the car. Our decision to move away from our child's home had immediate consequences for him too. He and his sister, born later, would forever be known as PKs, or preacher's kids, and that label brings its own story, best told from their perspective.

Driving that truck across windblown eastern New Mexico and the arid Texas panhandle on the road to an unknown future gave me more than enough time to revisit my decision to enter the seminary yet again. Was I making the right decision? This question reverberated throughout our family the next few years! I also returned again and again to another question that was asked a couple of years earlier, the one I heard so loudly: "Larry, have you thought about attending seminary?" How could a simple, casual inquiry open such a wide door to the option of pastoral ministry? I have always known there is power in the spoken word, and these words changed my life forever.

2

Family of Origin
—Shaping the Pastoral Identity

May those who sow in tears reap with shouts of joy. Those who go out weeping, bearing the seed for sowing shall come home with shouts of joy, carrying their sheaves.

—Ps 26:5–6

Journal Entry

There is a family legend passed down that claims when I was born, my two sisters, both teenagers at the time, were so excited they ran up one sidewalk and down the other in small downtown Julesburg shouting to anyone who cared to listen, "We have a baby brother!" Thank you for family.

UNDERSTANDING THE PASTORAL CALL and describing it to others is not simple. One reason for the complexity is the hidden dimension: family of origin. Family Systems Theory claims that much of our behavior—both constructive and destructive—results from the influences of our immediate and extended families. Mothers, fathers, siblings, aunts, uncles, cousins, grandparents, and great-grandparents all contribute to who we become as adults. Families heavily influence our character development, leadership qualities, life priorities, and understanding of God. This chapter will provide a small taste of the first biblical families, illustrating the generational impact of faith and behavior on generations that followed. Not dissimilarly, I will describe how my clan set the stage for a unique faith journey that eventually led to my pastoral call.

A four-inch-thick, black, leather-bound family Bible with our family tree inked in the front sat prominently on a living room end table in my childhood home. This genealogical tree began with my grandparents: Joseph and Martha and William and Sarah. One quick glance at it revealed where I fit in the family; my name was on the last line, filled in with my mother's beautiful cursive writing. When the pages of that massive family Bible opened to the first book of Genesis, the genealogy of other families were recorded. Rather than only bare lines with names, the biblical narrative was complete with the gritty details that make up all families.

FAMILIES OF THE BIBLE

After reading the patriarchal stories, one impression we are left with is shock; no detail of family dysfunction is spared. For example, the first recorded sibling relationship is between the estranged brothers Cain and Abel. Their conflict is so out of control that one brother goes so far as to take the life of the other (Gen 4)! The Bible doesn't linger long with these two brothers but quickly moves to the story of Abraham and Lot, two more struggling siblings (Gen 13). Rather than work the land together, they need to part ways. Abraham heads to the hills; Lot takes the fertile valley. Alienation persists to the next generation with the story of Isaac and Rebekah and their sons, Jacob and Esau. Jacob and his mother, Rebekah, trick Isaac into giving Jacob a patriarchal blessing rather than allow the blessing to be rightfully given to his older brother, Esau.

This problematic family system continues into the next generation as well when Jacob favors one of his sons at the expense of others. This early family tree illustrates how aberrant behavior in one child doesn't happen in isolation of the parents and grandparent's actions in earlier generations.

The biblical story with the longest and most detailed descriptions recording the impact of parents, grandparents, and siblings is the story of Jacob and his two wives, Rebecca and Leah, and their handmaidens, Bilhah and Zilpah (Gen 37–50). Joseph, son of Rebekah and Jacob, is a remarkable biblical character who used his family crisis to become a leader in Egypt, later saving his eleven brothers from starvation. Sold into slavery because of his brother's ill will toward him, Joseph not only survived, but prospered (Gen 15:15).

Growing through the trial and tribulations of family stress is always the goal, and family restoration invariably points the way toward unification with God. The story of Ruth is another account of family crisis turned into a story of overcoming. When Ruth states her intention to follow Naomi, her mother-in-law, back to Israel while leaving her own family behind, the power of God's reconciling love and compassion becomes apparent (Ruth 1:16–17). This beautiful book is dedicated to the saga of Ruth and her effort to enter a new family, one that has no place for an outsider. Generational records prove she not only became a member of her adopted family, but is also remembered in Scripture as a member of King David's as well as Jesus' genealogical lineage (Ruth 3:22).

The New Testament has a classic illustration of bad family behavior turned positive when family members chose to reconcile. The memorable account of the prodigal son and his forgiving father leaves the reader nearly stunned (Luke 15:11–32.) The forgiveness narrative is described in beautiful detail: "But while he was still far off, his father saw him and was filled with compassion; he ran and put his arms around him and kissed him" (Luke 15:20). There are unfinished family details in this story, but then again, all families have a sense of incompleteness to them, as their stories are still being written.

MY FAMILY

Making the transition from ancient families to my family seems like a giant leap, as mine seems peaceable by comparison, though certainly not perfect! As we see from the biblical families, however, the dynamics that play out can be the seedbed for either fertility and growth or alienation and pain. I believe pastors who are passionate about their vocational future need to wrestle a bit with the family influences that helped to shape their life and ultimately their ministry call. My assumption is that the more a candidate understands her family of origin, the more likely she will be in choosing the right congregation to complement her gifts. Likewise, she will be better equipped to comprehend the motivations that led her into this profession.

An unconscious but significant dimension into my call to pastoral ministry began with a compassionate mother and father who prioritized their Anabaptist Mennonite faith. They have traceable roots dating back to the early 1800s in the Alsace-Lorraine region of France. For the same reason my great-grandparents left Europe for a better life, so too did my parents, one hundred years later, depart a Mennonite stronghold in eastern Nebraska. They, like many during the time, were adversely affected by the economic conditions of the Great Depression and the infamous Dust Bowl.

Coming from a large farm family of twelve children, and following biblical precedent, the oldest son, my uncle Floyd, had first choice to inherit the family farm, leaving my father and his brothers with limited vocational options. As a result, my father, along with my mom and oldest sister, an infant at the time, packed up their belongings and moved to northeastern Colorado. There, my grandmother Sarah and her new second husband had recently relocated for the same economic reasons my parents had. My father and mother somehow scraped together a down payment to purchase a small acreage and a few dairy cows to begin their new vocation.

They immediately joined a small Mennonite congregation filled with others not unlike themselves—uprooted Mennonites transplanted to the high plains of western Nebraska and eastern Colorado. Located approximately thirty minutes from their newly adopted hometown of Julesburg, their stark white country church was surrounded by large dry-land wheat fields and a small fenced-off cemetery. In this place I formed my earliest memories of God's people gathering. With men sitting on one side of the sanctuary and women on the other, I alternated between Mom and Dad (as a child I was permitted on either side). Dad passed me small pieces of the black Lewis Brothers Cough Drops he always kept in his pocket to camouflage the stale cigarette smell that clung to him like the familiar odor of a well-cooked meal. Before church, he broke up the flavored cough drops with his ever-present pliers to make the supply last longer. He was, after all, a Dust Bowl survivor. Later in the service, after I moved across the aisle to sit with my mom, she made a lace hankie mouse that mysteriously ran up her arm. Both mom and dad entertained me while their eyes remained glued to the preacher, never once glancing down as they manipulated cough drops or lace-hankie mice. I also remember Sunday school in the country church basement, led by saintly women with large flannelgraph boards. Here, at the hands of these church mothers and grandmothers, Bible characters came to life as my early faith took root.

Later, when enough Mennonite families had migrated to Julesburg, Colorado, my parents' new home, the Julesburg Mennonite Church was formed. Unbeknownst to my nine-year-old-self, but nevertheless present like summer thunderclouds forming in the western sky was the stress felt in that old country church during the formation of a new congregation thirty miles away.

The church was central to the ordering of our family's weekly priorities. There was little, if any, understanding of the liturgical church calendar followed by our Catholic and Lutheran neighbors, but we did have an ordered church life predicated by Sunday morning and evening worship and Wednesday evening prayer meetings. I saw the same church members and their families at least three times a week. All of these congregational gatherings found our family at church singing, praying, and listening to the spoken Word.

In the fall after the crops were out of the ground, and in the spring before the farm irrigation water was needed, the bi-vocational bishop visited the new congregation to lead communion and foot washing services. He stayed in our home within the Pioneer Hotel, one of a number of businesses my parents had started. The Pioneer had thirty-three bedrooms where the bishop, overnight visitors, and long-term boarders stayed. Only a small door and the registration desk separated the hotel rooms from our living quarters. The visiting bishop frequently joined my parents and me for his meals. Church conversations around the dining room table were abundant, and, at times, entertaining.

I hold fond memories of life ordered around our small faith community. The annual Fourth of July picnic breakfast, held at the South Platte River Campground, made an indelible impression. With my eyes closed, I still smell cowboy coffee brewing with bacon and eggs frying on the fire pit. After breakfast, the pastor led us in devotions, often related to Jesus' Sermon on the Mount (Matt 5–7). We were, after all, non-resistant Christians, and this was the Fourth of July, a holiday promoting nationalism. The Sermon on the Mount provided the congregation a reminder of Christ's teachings on peace, a core belief. After the devotional, I remember playing among the river bottom cottonwood trees with friends as the adults talked and laughed.

Our family's late fall butchering ritual was a four-day event also etched in my memory. The normal routines were interrupted to process meat—part for us and a portion for the pastor's family. This "love offering" was for the pastor's service to the church. Since he received no set salary, members gave him cash in a designated monthly offering along with other tangible gifts throughout the year. When the stacks of the freshly wrapped meat were ready for the freezer, some were marked with a "P" to show they were the pastor's.

Most every evening I watched my father read his Bible while sitting in his favorite bent wood hickory rocker. The black leather

King James Bible on his lap looked worn. Though he had only an eighth grade education, he was a lifelong student of the Scriptures. Returning home over the holidays during my first year of college, he asked with a teasing twinkle in his eye, "What famous work of literature can you quote now that you're in college? Shakespeare?" The rhetorical question was followed with a pregnant pause as he waited for my response, which both of us knew would not be coming. Then, with perfect timing, he asked, "Can you quote the Bible?" Grinning before I could say anything else, he ended our "chat" with a King James Version verse like: "Study to show thyself approved unto God, a workman that needeth not to be ashamed, rightly dividing the word of truth" (2 Tim 2:15).

When it came time to decide about college, Dad was quite bold in his assertion that I should attend a Mennonite college. In fact, when I protested, saying I wanted to go where my friends were attending, a local state college, he gave an ultimatum: "If you want your mother's and my financial help, you'll attend a Mennonite college." I've often wondered about his motivation to speak so assertively about college. Was my father's stipulation that I go to a private, liberal arts, church college part of God's mystery, and thus part of my pastoral call? Unfortunately, my father died suddenly while I was away at school, leaving this question and many others left to my imagination.

My dad wasn't perfect, and I watched him struggle with the temptations of Christian living, one being his lifelong habit of rolling his own Bull Durham cigarettes. He went to extreme measures trying to stop, but never did conquer the addiction. His short temper, placated by my mother making sure our home life was organized and stress-free, was a daily reality. Through the rough-and-tumble of Christian life, however, Dad provided a foundation from which I could begin to construct my own Christian faith.

The primary parental presence in our home day in and day out was my mother. All her work seemed effortless, whether driving a school bus every morning and evening for twenty-four years, serving as the sole proprietor of the Pioneer Hotel, or managing the multiple rentals she and my father had accumulated. My mother is remembered as a competent businesswoman, faithful church worker, and loving homemaker. In each of those roles she exercised a belief that actions are a more valuable witness than words. When grapes were ripe and the rhubarb was ready to pick, a portion was always made into fresh juice and a little wine, served only on holidays.

In actuality, the Pioneer Hotel, which doubled as our home and business, was more like an inner city boarding house. The long-term residents of the hotel were either retired widowers or lifelong bachelors. Fifty dollars a month gave them a small hotel room, access to a hot plate for cooking, and a shared bathroom at the end of a long hallway. They treated me as a peer in conversations, and I played a lot of checkers with them in the hotel lobby. On most holidays, my mother would fix these hotel patrons a meal, and if one of the residents caught a bass or walleye at the local reservoir, Mom would prepare their catch, complete with mashed potatoes and corn on the cob.

I witnessed my mother's Christian patience put to the test many times when a patron pushed the limits of her forbearance with alcohol abuse, sexual promiscuity, or stealing. More than once I heard my mom tell an inebriated patron, "Go up to your room! You're being a nuisance." With the same kind of determination, I witnessed her chasing an "unregistered" woman from a guest's room. On occasion, a stranger tried breaking into the cash drawer under the registration counter, setting off a noisy bell. The bell, in turn, set off my mother's adrenalin. Jumping out of bed to throw on a robe, off she went, rushing into the hotel lobby to apprehend the intruder.

In the local congregation, Mom taught Sunday school classes, led a cappella congregational singing, and quilted blankets for family and charity. Even as she got older, teenagers saw a kindred spirit and frequently asked her to teach their class. These young people continue to recount how important she was in helping them negotiate their teenage years.

As previously noted, families are never confined to mother and father, sisters and brothers. Families also include grandparents and great-grandparents who carry not only the genetics, but also the family traditions, stories, and secrets. For instance, the stories of Grandma Sarah's unique spirit were common. She lost her husband, my grandfather William, to a blood infection too early in their marriage for him to help raise their four children. Yet, in spite of being a single parent, she took time to care for the sick in her community, including those in scarlet fever-quarantined homes. Sarah's inner strength and selfless giving in times of crisis during the early 1900s provided a role model for her children, including my mother.

Two grandparents, one on my mother's side and one on my father's side, were born out of wedlock—an embarrassment to them and a family secret carried in their close-knit communities. My grandfather William, in fact, never met his father, who supposedly had lived and worked in their community only a short time. When William learned at school that the grandparents raising him were not his real parents, he ran away from home for six months. His travel trunk sits in our guest bedroom and reminds me of his story.

Grandma Martha was born as the result of her mother, my great-grandmother, becoming pregnant as a very young woman. At the time of conception, she was cleaning the home of a married man in her church whose wife was bedridden. This great-grandfather later went on to become a Mennonite bishop. Martha carried a lasting embarrassment of being born out of wedlock, once introducing her mother as "aunt" Magdalena. Neither the bishop's family, nor my father or his siblings, knew of this family secret until the bishop's death and the reading of his will, which included his daughter Martha, my grandmother.

I have two siblings, spread out over seventeen years. Ask either of my two sisters, and they will confirm that I am the favored one, primarily because I'm the only male offspring and was an unexpected blessing. Family lore confirms the entire family's near euphoria at my birth. Married and out of the home before many of my early memories were formed, my sisters and their husbands felt more like parental figures. Fortunately, they were supportive surrogate parents and Christian role models I could emulate. My father was the obvious patriarch of this clan until his death. My mother seemed to move into the matriarch role almost effortlessly, and she continued to be the emotional glue that held us together.

FAMILY IMPLICATIONS FOR PASTORAL MINISTRY

Just as the ancient biblical stories demonstrate how one generation affects the other, my family likewise had a profound personal influence, including on my pastoral call. As the youngest of three children, yet raised as an only child, I developed a self-confidence that boded well when leadership skills later evolved. Though I seek approval of my peers, more so earlier than of late, the approval of others is secondary to standing with my convictions.

Raised with no siblings my age, I spent considerable time alone, which resulted in an enormous need for personal space. Groups in which I'm the center of attention sap my energy over time. Even though I have learned to be a charismatic and strong leader, time for recuperation and rejuvenation is vital for my mental and spiritual health.

There was an abundance of high-achieving, hard-working adults around me as I was growing up. Parents, grandparents, sisters, and brother-in-laws expected the same from me. All grown-ups in this circle of influence were creative, entrepreneurial, self-made, self-employed, and emotionally stable. I too am achievement-oriented, often to a fault. Give me an assignment, and I'll see that it's completed in a timely manner, with a sense of pride in a job done well. However, projecting my expectations onto others I'm working with can result in resentment if they don't work fast enough, demonstrate enough competence, or take the job as seriously as I think they should.

There were many formidable women in my life. They helped me, unconsciously, to feel a special link to equality and fairness related to women's issues. I had two older sisters, both of whom had opinions and were not afraid to express themselves, a high-achieving mother, and two grandmothers who overcame adversity. Early in my ministry, I chose to forgo, for eight years, my ordination until the first woman had been ordained in the conference in which I was employed.

The church was a significant part of my multigenerational family. In many ways, the local congregation was simply an extension of my family, and wanting to be part of the church was a natural outgrowth of the connection between family and church. There was little separation between them. This close linkage was extremely influential to my pastoral call.

However, the close relation between family and church was not always as it appeared on the surface. There were behavioral inconsistencies between what the church stood for and what my parents practiced, at least in a few areas. There were secrets embedded in two of my grandparents' births that also gave me perspective. What I learned was that the church's outward message sometimes contrasted sharply with some members' behavior. My family examples provided a healthy elasticity between my vocational calling and my personal identity, resulting in the faith community being more pliable than many others. Oftentimes, I'm suspicious of Christian behavior that is perceived as faultless.

There was a notable amount of tension between my father and mother. Much of their angst surrounded finances, even after they were no longer living hand-to-mouth. Watching my mother try to keep the peace (and she did a masterful job) provided me with the tools to placate and avoid conflict too, when necessary. However, those closest to me know I can be my father's son, especially when anxiety surrounding finances or unmet expectations causes me to be harsh.

Family stories help me to understand a pastoral call in the same way biblical stories help me to better appreciate how people of faith were formed. Likewise, a grasp of biblical family lineage and drama provides me with the courage, with God's grace, to use the grit and grist of my family circumstances to better construct and shape a pastoral career.

3

Conversion
—Laying a Foundation

For God so loved the world that he gave his only Son, so that everyone who believes in him may not perish but have eternal life.

—JOHN 3:16

Journal Entry

I remember responding to the pastor's invitation to raise my hand and come to the front of the sanctuary. What's less clear is why I raised my hand. What was my motivation? My "conversion" seemed less like a total turnaround than a mid-course adjustment.

A CONVERSION EXPERIENCE

WHEN I WAS FOURTEEN and a freshman in high school, I responded publically to an invitation to follow Christ. It happened one Sunday after my pastor's sermon: "With eyes closed and heads bowed, if anyone here feels God calling you to confess your sins and accept Jesus as your personal savior, please raise your hand." He then quoted Rom 6:23 from the King James Version: "For the wages of sin is death, but the free gift of God is eternal life in Jesus Christ our Lord." I hesitantly raised my hand, aware that a couple of other boys sitting beside me followed suit. Then the pastor requested that those of us who had raised our hands come forward to receive prayer. Three of us shyly walked to the front of the small sanctuary, which was filled that day, like most times the church gathered, with my mother, father, extended family, and a small band of other believers. Pastor Art thanked God for our decision to accept Jesus into our hearts and asked that our sins and life failures be forgiven. He closed, asking for our spiritual strength and a commitment to follow in the ways of Jesus.

I've heard many conversion stories as told from lifelong churchgoers, as well as from church dropouts. Guilt, peer pressure, and fear seem to be a common motivation for raising the "hand of salvation." However, when I publicly declared to God that I wanted to be a disciple, none of these emotions were a driving force behind the decision. In contrast, I felt led toward something positive and important. The community of faith—the local congregation—pulled me toward wanting to become a part of the larger whole. Raising my hand during the pastor's invitation was the beginning of that belonging process.

Since that day, I've thought more about my conversion experience, searching for a biblical role model. As I matured in my faith, Timothy's story, as told by the Apostle Paul, became the archetype for my own story. Second Timothy 1:5 reports that Timothy's mother and grandmother mentored him in a Christian home. His faith evolved out of that upbringing. He was, after all, a boy growing up in the shadow of the first-generation church, as his mother and grandmother would have been the first adults to encounter the good news. Timothy's conversion experience stands in contrast to that of the Apostle Paul, whose transformation was more startlingly dramatic. Paul describes his conversion as a blinding light in Acts 9:1–9. The light was so intense, he was without sight for three days, and the experience so vivid that he recounted the story twice more in Acts 22 and 26. Paul's conversion experience has unwittingly evolved as the primary Evangelical Christian model for describing how conversions happen.

New converts, for example, are often asked to describe their "bright light experience." Thus, most conversion stories sound something like this: "Before I was saved I was an addict" (or a thief, greedy, prideful, or mean). Hearing many of these changed life stories growing up, I came to the conclusion that my salvation experience wasn't authentic. Mine seemed to lack the radical about-face quality many Christians wanted to hear. Unfortunately, evangelical churches—my denomination included—often borrow more heavily from Paul's dramatic blinding light conversion experience than from Timothy's in-home Christian metamorphosis.

The following detail about how I came to raise my hand that one day, so many years ago, seems important to share. A few weeks prior to responding to my pastor's invitation, I asked my father in the privacy of our home, "Dad, how do I get baptized?" My father responded by describing the sequence of events leading to baptism and said he would speak with the pastor to see that I received an "invitation." I later figured out that the "invitation" would come in the form of an "altar call," at which time the pastor would invite me to the "altar," and he would pray with me. However, in my church sanctuary there was no altar, only a row of *Sansevieria trifasciata* plants, more commonly known as Mother-in-Law's Tongue, which served to demarcate the pews from the pulpit area. It was to those plants I walked on that "Invitation Sunday" so long ago. I do not recall our pastor making other salvation invitations similar to mine, which probably speaks to the infrequency of young people or guests in our worship.

In contrast to my experience, I recall—from the times I visited—the frequent altar calls at the Nazarene Church my sister attended in a neighboring community. I have a particularly vivid memory of watching my sister, a stalwart leader in that congregation, walk to the front of the sanctuary to kneel at the clearly demarcated altar rail, while the congregation sang "Just as I Am."

I was perplexed as to why she needed to go forward, since she had long ago been baptized. I learned later that walking to the front rail, at least for the Nazarenes, serves a variety of purposes, receiving a pastoral prayer being one.

In my denomination, going forward set in motion a sequence of events, including a series of instruction classes for new believers and faith-related questions to be answered in a new believer's instruction book. A service of baptism was planned for six months later so that family members living at a distance could attend.

During my baptismal service, Pastor Art reminded the congregation of the meaning of baptism—that it was an outward symbol of a personal and inner commitment, and also the entry point, so to speak, into the local congregation. Baptism opened the door to full fellowship and participation, including the taking of bread and juice during communion. This was in keeping with our denominational theology at that time.

While kneeling, Pastor Art poured water over my head. Then, firmly placing his hands on my wet hair, he requested the infilling of the Holy Spirit. The same ritual was performed for three other new converts—all high school boys—as they bowed their heads in the chancel that Sunday morning. The building was silent, a kind of quietness that resembles the pause before a good storyteller delivers a climactic conclusion. At that moment, I had entered the historic stream of Christian believers, including five thousand of the early Anabaptists—my forebears—who were subject to martyrdom for this very same act of adult Christian baptism. Although some would argue that the age of fourteen hardly gave me adult status, I did voluntarily make this decision, answering a quiet, yet distinctive and individual call to follow Christ.

After the pastoral prayer of blessing, I rose from my knees, and forty members of this devout faith community filed up to the *Sansevieria trifasciata* and welcomed me, along with two other new believers. This event continues to hold a sacred place in my memory, serving as a signpost along the faith journey, marking the time of an outward sign of an invisible grace. Family and friends, mostly adults, gave a hug, offered a hand of fellowship, or planted a kiss on my cheek. I left feeling embarrassed for the tears that welled up in my eyes. There was no doubt that day, or today, that I became part of a historic Anabaptist faith community identified as Mennonite, and also a member of the larger ecumenical Christian community. This formative experience helped shape my sense of a pastoral call and expectation for what the church could offer children and youth—a sense of belonging and friendship that lasts a lifetime.

PERSONAL AWARENESS

Skip forward with me twenty-plus years. In that span, there was enough time to complete high school, go to college, get married, father a child, begin a vocation, move a few times, go to seminary, change vocations, and become a pastor.

Strange as it might sound, as a pastor I did not use this same model to invite others to faith. My resistance to inviting congregants to raise their hands as a sign of repentance and contrition was further confirmed after preaching a number of times at the local Rescue Mission. A neighboring congregation had a monthly commitment to lead worship and preach there, and the pastor of this church frequently called on me to cover for him when he had other obligations. The evening routine began with homeless men walking into the mission off the street at dusk, then taking part in a worship service planned by host congregations. Following a service that included singing, Scripture reading, and a salvation-oriented sermon, the men received a meal and a bed for the night. This had been the Rescue Mission's operational model since 1942. The first time I preached there, I was surprised to see a small metal sign screwed to the pulpit, visible only to the preacher standing behind it. In all caps it read, "FOLLOWING THE SERMON, AN INVITATION TO ACCEPT CHRIST SHALL BE GIVEN."

My first sermon there was quickly adapted to include an invitation for the men to raise their hands and come forward for prayer. One puffy-eyed man, looking to be in his late 50s, raised his hand and hesitantly walked to a small front altar area. I stepped forward from the pulpit to meet him but quickly discovered his intoxication. The smell of alcohol permeated my senses, and for a moment I was drawn back to my childhood home in the Pioneer Hotel, where alcoholics were not uncommon. I ushered the slightly inebriated man off to the side of the sanctuary and signaled others to close the service with a song and a prayer. After praying with the stranger, he shyly asked if I could give him a few dollars.

All the men seemed hungry and tired, and I assumed, for right or wrong, they needed a meal more than my call to repentance. I preached at the mission a few more times before telling the pastor for whom I was substituting that he would need to find a different pulpit supply in the future.

My discomfort in asking people for a raised hand or to come forward in worship as a way to demonstrate a contrite heart and willingness to accept Jesus continued. One reason for my uneasiness was the dissonance I felt with my early teenage conversion experience. Even with all the positive emotion I experienced the day I raised my hand and in the baptism that followed, there were many years of Christian lifestyle challenges that followed. The inconsistency between my decision to raise a hand and go forward to signal my conversion compared with my seemingly unchristian actions later on made me doubt the authenticity of my experience.

These symbolic gestures at age fourteen did not insulate me from the pressures to conform and the temptations that came in high school, college, and early adulthood. I had little theological grounding for understanding the incongruity between the promises I made at conversion and the breaking of those promises so soon after. As a result, I felt confused and guilty during much of my young adult life.

By the time I went to seminary, those confusing feelings had subsided, though not disappeared. A college degree specializing in education had given me the language to describe my emotions and better understand people's developmental stages. I learned too that children are best taught according to age appropriateness and developmental readiness. When I applied this concept to my conversion experience, I realized my immaturity and lack of perspective. As a fourteen-year-old child, I had neither the readiness for religious training nor the ability to comprehend a public acknowledgment of sin. Admitting my sinful life and then promising to live a holy life set the stage for a Christian life with confounding emotions.

In hindsight, I think I would have been better served if a mentor had been assigned to me following those early questions I asked my father about church membership. An adult providing me guidance over a longer period of time, followed by eventual baptism, would have been more appropriate to my age and stage. The church's emphasis on coming forward to acknowledge sin didn't fit my experience or my theological readiness. Some might say that the church may risk missing opportunities for retaining its youth if it forgoes the opportunity to baptize at a young age. In fact, I've had many conversations with well-intentioned Christians who have no qualms in leading children much younger than fourteen to Christ. This model of childhood evangelism, which emphasizes conversion from a life of sin, never fit my theological experience, nor was it something I wanted to encourage.

Beginning with Charles G. Finney and continuing with Dwight L. Moody and, more recently, with Billy Graham, evangelists of the mid to late 1800s made the invitation to come forward as a sign of repentance and request for forgiveness the climax of each worship service in their mass evangelical crusades. Influenced by the zeal of these evangelists, my denomination began a similar emphasis. This became the preferred method of bringing the unsaved and children to Christian faith. I hasten to add that there is biblical precedent in Acts 2:41 for a crusade-type atmosphere. Here Luke writes, "So those who welcomed his message were baptized, and that day about three thousand persons were added."

The New Testament gives other examples, however, of how individuals come to faith. Jesus frequently called individuals into a personal relationship with him, and his calls seemed tailor-made, as if they had a personal fit. His invitations were also appropriate to each situation. He spoke about little children and used them as examples of how adults should have faith (Matt 19:14). He called

Zacchaeus down from a tree and invited himself to dinner (Luke 19:1–10). He spoke directly, yet without condemnation, to a harlot (John 8:1–11). Jesus also called twelve disciples (Matt 10:1–4), but each man's invitation was specific and personalized.

A NEW MODEL

What I discovered early in pastoral ministry was that most people coming to worship fell into two categories: either adults with some kind of previous faith experience or children brought along because of their parents. I don't recall any individuals entering the church's doors who were entirely new to the Christian faith. In fact, most visiting adults were dropouts from other Christian denominations. Some who found their way back to church indicated interest in rededicating their life to Christ, and I re-baptized them.

Without hesitation, I can say that all new attenders were searching for something missing in their spirituality or prior church experience. Often their faith was not as strong, personal, helpful, or dynamic as they wanted, or their relationship to Christ needed to be repaired and rekindled. Some came because of a gap between their faith and the teachings in the church they had left; their faith simply wasn't working for them anymore. But what exactly they were looking for in this new setting became a process of pastoral discovery. This pastoral journey of discovery with people helped to define my sermons and worship experiences. Encouraging congregants towards a maturing faith and providing a language to express that faith became a priority in our corporate worship times and in private pastoral conversation.

The method of calling people to a deeper relationship with Christ became organic, more directly tied to the preaching text on a given Sunday. For example, a sermon related to the Gospel story of the lost coin (Luke 15:8–10) concluded with a responsive reading of reclaiming a misplaced or forgotten belief in Christ. A sermon on Exodus related to the desert wanderings and complaining ended with a congregational response seeking forgiveness. On occasion, I invited anyone who wanted prayer and the laying on of hands (Jas 5:14) to come to the side of the sanctuary, where a lay leader prayed with them. I think the urban context and the member demographics attracted to the congregation helped me shape a method of sharing the gospel that was relevant and transformative.

The congregation developed a custom of pairing every eleven-to-fourteen-year-old with a spiritually mature adult. This mentoring relationship was intended to be ongoing throughout the teenage years and into early adulthood. The mentor's role was to guide the young person in his or her search for spiritual meaning, ultimately leading, if they chose, to a commitment to Christ followed by baptism. This process seemed more fitting, age appropriate, and congruent with my understanding of how best to initiate a Christian call to children of the church. Yet being a pastor to a diverse group required me to remain flexible and adapt at times to other wishes.

When an occasional parent wanted their child baptized earlier than I thought appropriate, a pastoral conversation was initiated. One couple from Lutheran and Catholic backgrounds wanted to have their baby baptized in the same religious tradition as their parents. Following a pastoral discussion and extensive reading on the subject of adult versus childhood baptism, they chose to have their baby, and the babies that followed, baptized at the local Lutheran church when the grandparents came to town for a visit. In another situation, an anxious father called late at night to criticize me for not wanting to baptize his two children, then aged nine and eleven: "They need to be covered in the blood. If you don't baptize them, I'll do it in the bathtub." Two years later, after undergoing instruction and a mentor relationship, I baptized both children in the local river, with all of us wearing the flowing white gowns expected by the father.

When I began this chapter, I stated that conversion stories are often limited to "bright light" experiences like the Apostle Paul's. What I've discovered, however, is that the call to become a Christ follower is ongoing and unending. Conversion is a process of faith discovery. As the Apostle Paul says in Phil 2:12–13, "work out your own salvation with fear and trembling; for it is God who is at work in you, enabling you both to will and to work for his good pleasure." Everyone has a unique faith journey. There is no one-size-fits-all conversion experience. Being at ease with my beginning of my call of God took many years of reading, processing, studying, and observing. Only later did I finally accept my conversion as valid. The essence of the pastoral call is meeting people where they're at on the journey of faith and welcoming them as partners as the process of conversion continues. The call to pastoral ministry is no different; it is a lifelong journey of faith.

4

The Interview
—Choosing a Pastor

But the Lord said to Samuel, "Do not look on his appearance or on the height of his stature, because I have rejected him; for the Lord does not see as mortals see; they look on the outward appearance, but the Lord looks on the heart."

—1 SAM 16:7

Journal Entry

Wow! I forgot how much I missed living out West. The sky is a deep blue and the cloud formations so vivid. The open spaces allow me to take a deep breath. Am I coming home? I want this interview to go well. Could God be calling me here?

THE CIRCLE IS SMALL: three women and two men. Most look to be near my age, although one gray-haired woman appears to be a generation older. They have gathered this warm spring evening to interview me. I'm a twenty-nine-year-old seminary student—almost ready to graduate—and these kind folks are looking for a pastor. I've traveled from the sacred halls of higher learning "in the East" to meet this small group "out West." We are courting, so to speak. They want to know if I am going to match the pastor profile they have so diligently created, and I am wondering if this is where I want to begin a pastoral career. Moreover, I am still asking if God has, for sure, called me to be a pastor.

Following the usual small talk related to travel itineraries, we did what new groups tend to do; we searched for common links to make the transition into deeper dialogue a bit easier. Surely we could find a mutual friend or family member, a church connection, or some similar experiences to help us get acquainted. Fortunately, it didn't take long before we found some links that seemed to put us more at ease. These communal connections are significant in establishing an early bond, especially in smaller religious traditions. After our exchange related to mutual acquaintances, the "real" interview began. The chairperson started the conversation by giving a welcome: "We are delighted you've chosen to visit. Some of us seem to know you better than others. In order for us all to get better acquainted, each of the committee members has prepared a question in hopes of learning about your thoughts and ideas related to ministry. After each asks their question, we invite your response. We want you to relax. Consider us all like a family."

"A family? What does that mean?" I thought. Families do not interview one another, and if they did, some family members would not have been given the title of uncle, aunt, brother, sister, or cousin. No, this pastoral interview does not feel like family. A boy visiting his girlfriend's parents for the first time is a better comparison. I felt nervous.

"Have you ever spoken in tongues?" "What do you believe about the gifts of the Holy Spirit?" These were the first two questions. I stuttered to make an intelligent response, but I don't recall what I said. Certainly, this gathering was in no way similar to any family event I could remember. For one thing, our clan spoke little about controversial topics. The last time we had talked religion, my sister blurted out, "Why do you always have to be so different?" This rhetorical question was not intended as a compliment, and led in part to my observation that advanced theological degrees can create suspicion between a pastor and some laity by producing theological conversational gaps. One reason might be that a seminary prepares students to think critically, not unlike college in general. In my seminary classes, for instance, I learned about biblical criticism, a method of Bible study that attempts to interpret Scripture by examining its historical, cultural, and contextual background. I also learned that analytical thinking does not make for spontaneous or easy responses. As counterintuitive as this may sound, seminary education made answering theological questions more difficult! The two questions posed at the beginning of my interview made me stumble for a response, as they seemed too complex to answer quickly

Later, in congregational ministry, a congregant might have asked a question like, "How can you say war is wrong when the Old Testament is full of war stories?" My response might have sounded dismissive, but it was never intended as such. I simply could not give a pat answer. Rather, I would respond, "That is a great question. Can we talk about it in more detail over coffee?" This rejoinder often seemed less than satisfactory to the questioner, however, and I assumed that seminary was implicated for making the Bible too complex. What I sometimes forgot to consider in these situations was whether a question was actually a question or simply a way to express an opinion.

As stated earlier, the two Holy Spirit-oriented interview questions left me rattled. Later in my ministry, however, I found relevance to those questions and used the critical thinking tools gained in seminary to better understand the person behind the question. The often-heard phrase at that time, "speaking in tongues," became, for me, an appropriate metaphor to describe the various spiritual languages spoken in my congregation. Thus, I would benefit from learning a range of spiritual dialects, since each person related to me through the window and language of their spiritual experience. For instance, one congregant suggested I "think too much" in my sermon preparation. "You need to set your brain aside and let the Holy Spirit guide you," was her unsolicited advice. She was speaking with a strong charismatic dialect. The member who asked me, "Why don't you preach more from the book of Revelation and Daniel?" wanted me to speak his language of eschatology. The congregant who told me I should have more invitations to accept Christ after my sermons, was using her evangelical language. The humanitarian political activist, on the other hand, pointed out that she was uncomfortable with the heavy emphasis on Jesus in sermons, song, and testimony.

Pity the linguistically challenged pastor who cannot easily recognize and speak the numerous spiritual dialects! At the time of my interview, I was too immature to recognize many of these underlying interests. Instead, I was dumbfounded by my inability to answer questions quickly and with authority, quoting Scripture and verse. Ironically, my interview with the search committee was cut short because of a robbery in the vicinity of the church building. Supposedly, the robber was hiding in the parsonage garage, and we were told by the investigating police to evacuate the building.

Before leaving the interview topic, however, I wonder just what the best way to learn about a candidate's theological orthodoxy might be. A candidate can answer both theological and doctrinal questions to the search committee's satisfaction and still not have a successful ministry. Perhaps a denomination's screening process, coupled with a clear credentialing policy, is the optimal path for exploring a candidate's theological orthodoxy in detail. As part of the denomination's call process, pastor peers and others skilled at reading pastor applications usually examine a candidate's theological orientation. This approach can be extremely helpful to a congregation even before the candidate and congregation engage one another in a face-to-face conversation. Extensive questioning related to specific Christian doctrine will be more of a necessity in independent congregations, where there may not be a denominational call system in place.

The pastoral interview, important as it seems to both the candidate and the search committee, actually has limited use in determining a good fit between congregation and pastoral candidate. The interview gives a glimpse, not a complete picture, of whether there is potential for a relationship. Other aspects of the on-site visit are important too. In-home meals, sightseeing trips with members, small group meetings, and informal conversations give both the candidate and congregation additional peepholes; each provides an opening to discern God's voice for the future of the relationship.

Another part of the congregational visit that weighs heavily for or against issuing a pastoral call is the candidate's sermon. This sermon is a momentous ritual for both the congregation and the pastor. Congregations struggle to find appropriate tools to evaluate a candidate's fit, and the sermon is one of these, but it need not be a decisive indicator. As important as preaching is to the life of most congregations, preaching styles and methodology change over time. Most preachers improve their sermon delivery, becoming more creative with experience.

When I nervously walked into the door of the sanctuary to preach my candidate sermon, I expected to see a pulpit and rows of chairs. What I encountered was a circle of chairs beginning to fill in with adults and a few squirming children. Since there was no pulpit, my anxiety was heightened. "What am I going to do with the precious sermon notes I so carefully prepared ahead of time? My lap isn't big enough to hold the Bible and notes!" Normally these preaching aids are organized neatly on the pulpit to be referenced or read during the twenty- to twenty-five-minute sermon. I needed to adapt quickly in what would be the first of many preaching format, setting, and style changes I would need to adjust to throughout my ministry.

Apart from the more obvious activities scheduled when a candidate visits the congregation, including the formal interview and sermon, there are other considerations that I refer to as "cultural connecting points." For instance, I've often noted a gap between an urban versus a rural church experience. A candidate with rural pastoral experience might have difficulty relating to the cultural differences in an urban congregation, and of course, the opposite may be true as well. Another cultural connecting point is the educational parity between pastor and congregation. As mentioned earlier, a pastor who holds advanced degrees can be a barrier to some in the congregation. The converse is also true: a congregation with highly educated members will expect a pastor to have a similar educational vita. Also, the gender of the candidate can make the adjustment difficult. If a candidate is the first woman a congregation has considered for pastoral leadership, this change might prove challenging for some. The same point can be made for any differences, including sexual orientation, race, or ethnicity. Thus, both the pastor candidate and congregation need to be particularly sensitive in negotiating their relationship. I hasten to add that dissimilarities alone should never be a sole reason to reject a candidate. Discriminating against a candidate because or age, disability, race, gender, marital status, or sexual orientation is always wrong.

A congregation intent on prioritizing its cultural and ethnic diversity can emphasize interviewing candidates with specific expertise. A congregation might ask a candidate about his vision for expanding diversity in the church, his history working cross-culturally, or about his international mission or development experience.

In Gal 3:28, the Apostle Paul writes, "There is no longer Jew or Greek, there is no longer slave or free, there is no longer male and female; for all of us are one in Christ Jesus." Apostle Paul's vision of the church is beautiful and inspiring. In many congregations, however, Paul's vision needs attention and intention by congregational leaders and pastors if it is ever to be a reality.

To be frank, I found growing a congregation with so much diversity to be a challenge. The urban congregation I pastored had a young, professional, politically progressive member roster. We had a difficult time retaining blue-collar workers, senior citizens, the politically conservative, or people of color. Rather, we attracted and kept more people like ourselves—certainly not the diversity described by the Apostle Paul.

Apart from any of the pastoral search topics already addressed, I believe assessing a candidate's relational intelligence to be crucial. More than a few challenges will exist for a pastor and congregation if the pastor has difficulty bonding with parishioners. Relationship-oriented pastors take a genuine interest in others; they ask questions and then listen—really well. They tend to remember bits and pieces of a conversation and later ask a follow-up question. Relationally intelligent pastors love to hear stories and are capable of sharing appropriate personal stories in turn to build emotional connections. A pastoral search committee needs to ask, "Is this candidate someone our congregation can relate to?" as well as, "Do we find this candidate easy to talk to?"

One pastor friend had a terrible time remembering names, but he compensated by frequently acknowledging the shortcoming. People simply knew this to be one of pastor's "funny quirks." Even though my friend might forget a member's name, he would attend a high school music concert when a youth from his congregation was performing, then talk with that young woman about her experience. Members loved him despite this glaring relationship challenge.

Another pastor was a social introvert, preferring to read a book than mingle with people. However, he remembered small details of a congregant's life and asked about the specifics when the right moment presented itself. This pastor could also be funny, turning shyness into a dry sense of humor at unusual moments. A pastor lacking this kind of emotional connectivity to engage members or guests in meaningful ways will have a difficult time building long-term relationships.

Calling a candidate's references is important, but again, checking a reference is only one tool in the discernment process. Most references are close friends and peers who will likely give a positive spin on the candidate's character and abilities. There is no substitute for learning to know the candidate independently from his or her references. One candidate listed a respected high-profile pastor as a reference. The influence of this one reference overshadowed other parts of the candidate's profile that were more problematic. Although the candidate was ultimately invited to serve, the new pastor/congregation relationship lasted only a few years.

As may be evident from this chapter, calling a pastor is not an exact science. I liken the pastoral call process to unraveling a kind of divine mystery, much as the prophet Elijah tried to comprehend God's presence while standing in the mouth of the cave he was hiding in (1 Kgs 19:11–13). Because of this divine mystery, the process that surrounds the call between pastor and congregation deserves reverence. Both the pastoral candidate and the faith community must pay close attention to where the Holy Spirit of God might be leading, for they are involved in an ancient yet timeless ritual—that of discerning leadership. First Samuel 16:7 recounts a small but crucial detail in the story of how the future King David was chosen. This verse reads, "But the Lord said to Samuel, 'Do not look on his appearance or on the height of his stature . . . for the Lord does not see as mortals see; they look on the outward appearance, but the Lord looks on the heart.'" As the astute reader knows, Samuel eventually chose David. He alone seemed to know God's intention.

Choosing a pastor is seldom as straightforward as it was for Samuel, especially in denominations where organizational polity allows individual congregations to make their own pastoral invitation. The congregation, in these situations, needs to answer the question, "Is God leading our congregation to invite this person to be our pastor?" The candidate, in turn, responds to the question, "Is God calling me to this congregation?" Ultimately, these questions are answered in the subjective world of personal and corporate discernment. As much as the congregation might have a list of objective criteria to check off in order to make the "right" decision, clarity is often evasive. Thus, they turn to more subjective questions in discernment: Do those who have met the candidate feel engaged and emotionally connected to the candidate? Is there a sense of excitement and energy from both the candidate and the congregation? Is there a feeling of peace about calling this candidate to lead our congregation? When the responses to questions like these are affirmative, they provide a sense of the Spirit's leading towards a decision. The congregation is given the confidence that God has indeed been in the process.

My first letter of invitation to serve as pastor was momentous. I was filled with both joy and fear. My budding pastoral call was affirmed. I wanted to be a pastor for this congregation, and the small church plant also wanted me! Yet I had a fear of failing to live up to expectations—both theirs and mine. I lived with these uncertainties for the next number of years.

How closely was the congregational invitation to become a pastor linked to my pastoral call from God? What if the congregation had chosen someone else instead? How would I have interpreted their decision? It's hard to say, but hopefully I would have continued the discernment process with another congregation. Jesus told his disciples, "If anyone will not welcome you or listen to your words, shake off the dust from your feet as you leave that house or town" (Matt 10:14). I use this passage as a metaphor to describe a possible response when a gift is offered but rejected. Sometimes the relational chemistry is simply not right between a congregation and candidate. When the on-site congregational visit does not culminate with a call, my suggestion to both parties is the same: Continue to pray for guidance, listen for God's leading, and move on! God will provide other opportunities.

5

Congregations Aren't Equal
—Finding the Right Fit

To the angel of the church in Ephesus write . . . And to the angel of the church in Syrna write . . . And to the angel of the church in Pergamum write . . . And to the angel of the church in Thyatira write . . . And to the angel of the church in Sardis write . . . And to the angel of the church in Philadelphia write . . . And to the angel of the church in Laodicea write.

—REV 2:1A, 8A, 12A, 18A, 3:1A, 7A, 14A

Journal Entry

There is no doubt God has called me to this congregation. After all, I did my homework! But—and there is always a but—why do some of the people who were so eager for me to come now show such so little excitement to build this faith community?

THE PASTOR CHOOSING THE right congregation is just as significant as the pastoral discernment process described in the last chapter. Validation of a pastoral call is taken one step further when a local congregation extends an invitation to the candidate. However, the process is not complete until the pastor accepts their invitation. Because not all congregations are equal in their ability to form and sustain a healthy bond with a pastor, the pastoral candidate does well to explore the congregation's life story and its current trajectory with all the intensity of an athlete in training, for the stakes are high. While some congregations are nurturing and mission-driven, allowing the pastor to partner with them, other congregations remain entangled in unhealthy legacies with a resulting history of short-term pastors.

While a congregation has the ability to shape and reinforce a pastoral call, the pastor has a significant influence as well on the life and ministry of the congregation. Imagine the disappointment and pain for both, then, if they do not meet one another's expectations and the relationship ends badly.

Before going into more detail about varying congregational dynamics, I want to acknowledge the existence of two prominent, yet very different, pastoral call systems. One is congregationally-centered, while the other is bishop-centered. In this and the previous chapter, I describe a congregationally-based polity in which the congregation chooses its pastor and the pastor chooses a congregation. In the bishop-centered pastoral call system, a bishop who is outside the local congregation assumes a major role in pastoral placement. While each arrangement has advantages and disadvantages, neither system is superior or more biblical than the other. Each can be effectual when clear policy and qualified people guide the process.

As a denominational executive for many years, as well as an ecumenical consultant, I can bear witness to the difficulties that emerge between congregations and pastors regardless of the call system. Unfortunately, when the pastor/congregation relationship doesn't work, pastors seldom stay in professional ministry. Congregations suffer as well after a difficult separation from their pastor and are not likely to recover quickly. The toll that conflict takes on all involved—congregations, pastors, and the pastor's family—is considerable.

EVALUATING A CONGREGATION

There is good news, however! Many loving and caring congregations exemplify what the Apostle Paul describes in Eph 2:19–22:

> So then you are no longer strangers and aliens, but you are citizens with the saints and also members of the household of God, built upon the foundation of he apostles and prophets, with Christ Jesus himself as the cornerstone. In him the whole structure is joined together and grows into a holy temple in the Lord; in whom you also are built together spiritually into a dwelling place for God.

Is there anywhere in Scripture where the church and all its moving parts are more beautifully described?

Based on this illustrative passage, five values emerge that can help a pastor candidate assess a congregation's priorities. These values should form the foundation of the congregation's vision and mission:

- Jesus Christ: A prominent Christology motivates all activities and is evident throughout the congregation's worship and structure.

- Relationships: There are no strangers or aliens. The language of inclusion is commonplace.

- Training and Education: Programs exist for training new congregational leaders and believers, and educating people of all ages in the ways of Christ. There are ample opportunities to learn and grow together.

- Connectedness: The congregation participates in the regional, national, and global faith community structures. There is an awareness the local church is part of something greater.

- Growth and Change: The congregation is a dynamic, growth-oriented body and has a way to measure its effectiveness in all areas of its ministry.

Many differences exist in how congregations do or do not embody these values. The seven churches mentioned in chapters 2 and 3 of Revelation illustrate this congregational diversity. Each congregation listed has a unique story describing its faithfulness, or lack thereof. The writer of Revelation praises some while giving others a failing grade, and a few receive a combination of both praise and criticism. For instance, the church at Ephesus is known for hard work and perseverance. Read the stories of each of the seven congregations, and one finds both indictment and praise.

At the time the book of Revelation was written, each of the seven congregations had developed seventy-five years of historical narrative, not unlike many North American congregations today. Like churches today, they each had a distinct personality, along with their own peculiar strengths and weaknesses.

As stated earlier, to accept or not accept a specific congregation's invitation to serve as pastor is not a simple decision. Along with other factors, each congregation's individual history and story needs to be considered: When and why was the church started? What was the vision of the founding families and the first pastor? What do current leaders know about the congregation's history? When did the congregation come to occupy its current physical space and location? What is the average tenure of former pastors? Which organizational conflicts were handled well, and which ones still linger? Where does the congregation's passion lie? Congregations that are self-aware can often articulate what they have learned from past mistakes. Congregations with less insight about their past, however, might have difficulty responding to a candidate's inquiry about their history and be more inclined to repeat past mistakes.

Where does a candidate considering a call to a specific congregation begin getting their questions answered aside from the questions they ask directly to congregation leaders? Awareness begins with reading the congregational profile or a similar information sheet. Most congregations will be required to complete a self-portrait if they are part of a denomination and participating in a regional call process. From the congregational profile, the candidate can learn the average attendance, group demographics, leadership structure, financial status, building details, and congregational priorities. This description is the first and most important window for viewing the congregation. After gathering this information, the candidate would do well to engage in personal reflection. Candidates might ask themselves, "Does the church and community seem like a place I could have a meaningful ministry? Are people enthused and invested in the congregation? Does their mission resonate with my personal sense of God's call?" Likewise, "Can the budget realistically support a pastor, plus their other ministries?" And most importantly, "Are the five values evident in Eph 2:19–22 noticeable?"

Another resource for the candidate is the conference minister or bishop. Regional judicatories bring a wealth of information and wisdom to the congregational placement. They are pastors with expertise in the call system and understand the congregations in their charge. With good fortune, a pastoral candidate will develop a meaningful relationship with this person and benefit greatly from his or her insights and judgment. For instance, if there seemed to be a short tenure between pastors, the district pastor might be able to give perspective and respond to questions such as "Did the former pastor resign out of a sense of call or because of congregational unrest?"

Every congregational search committee should have a chairperson who will be the candidate's primary contact until an invitation to visit the congregation for a personal interview is extended. The chairperson's responsibility is to provide information and be a portal into the congregation. Numerous phone calls and exchanges between the candidate and the search committee chairperson are not uncommon. If there is a divine spark between the chairperson and the candidate, the flame of excitement begins to burn. Sharing ideas for ministry and mission further fans the embers of enthusiasm between the candidate and chairperson.

In an ideal situation, the candidate and chairperson are practicing spiritual discernment. Both are keeping notes of their conversations and documenting their feelings and questions. Each is continuously asking God for divine wisdom and insight. The search committee representative is keeping other members informed of the process and requesting prayer. The candidate is likewise consulting with family and friends, expanding ownership of the ultimate decision. The search committee is calling pastoral references. Combined, these intentional practices for seeking a sacred wisdom will give confidence when the time comes to say yes or no to an invitation to visit the congregation.

A CASE STUDY

What follows is a description of the congregational history and dynamics at play before I accepted a call to my first pastorate, Hyde Park Mennonite. Even though the small group of worshipers were calling themselves a new church startup—sometimes referred to as a church plant—I quickly discovered in my initial conversations with church leaders that this was actually a second startup attempt. The first try had taken place six years earlier.

I learned that leaders in a small town congregation called First Church—located twenty-five miles away—had "planted" this new congregation in the neighboring city's historic core, Hyde Park. This initial church planting effort ended with misunderstandings and stressed relationships, both at First Church and at Hyde Park Mennonite. Unfortunately, a great deal of time, energy, monetary resources, volunteer labor, and goodwill had been expended to get this new church off to a good start during the original attempt, only to be met with a sense of failure.

The depth of the misunderstanding between leaders at First Church and Hyde Park Mennonite dribbled out as I conducted my "background check." The actual distance separating the old and new congregations was less than thirty miles, but this geographical separation was miniscule compared to the gap between the two groups' missional understandings of what it means to plant a church in an urban setting.

Even though both congregations shared similar values, as referenced earlier in Eph 2:19–22, the missional visions that emerged were very different. First Church had purchased a vacant, historic Evangelical Friends church building to help kick-start the new urban congregation. A pastor was called, and he and his family moved to the city to live near the new Hyde Park church building. After the new pastor was on-site, he decided to renovate the old building's sanctuary. Sloping floors were leveled, old oak benches were either sold or given away, and a donated pool table was set up in the basement. The new startup envisioned Hyde Park Mennonite as a youth community center that would double as a worship facility on Sunday, but First Church had a vision of a more traditional church—one that would look something like their own.

Another example of competing visions was Hyde Park Mennonite's decision to promote and lead military draft counseling classes for young men. During the height of the Vietnam War, these draft counseling classes became front-page news for the local paper, resulting in even more dissention between the new church and First Church. The counseling classes were considered a "ministry opportunity" and a "bold new vision" by the startup church. First Church thought of the classes as "radical" and "too political." While "radical" or "political" are not necessarily bad monikers for a Mennonite congregation, they were labels that festered among key leaders of the First Church.

Further complicating matters between the two congregations was the conflict emerging among First Church's own membership. Lines were drawn between those who supported the new church plant and those who did not. The fallout of this rift resulted in a number of families leaving First Church. Financial giving from First Church in support of their church plant in Hyde Park dwindled, making it difficult for the Hyde Park Mennonite's pastor to continue. He eventually resigned. Finally, in a bold but exasperated move, First Church gave the church plant project—including their ownership of the building—to the broader Mennonite denomination, eager to put this good idea gone so badly in their past. The denomination was left with the building, a small mortgage, and the remnants of a burning vision to begin a Mennonite church in the city. Fortunately, this ember was kept alive by some additional Mennonites who migrated to the city and surrounding area to pursue jobs and college.

IMPLICATIONS

One might ask, "Are congregational dynamics like the one just described unusual?" I believe there are many comparable stories. One reason this particular account may sound familiar is its similarity to Gal 2, in which the Apostles Paul and Peter have a dispute over expectations of the church in Jerusalem for the new church in Galatia. The astute pastoral candidate will often uncover some form of conflict that helped birth the specific congregation she is interviewing. She needs to stay mindful, because a history of conflict will remain a part of the congregation's institutional memory long into the future and will often influence the congregation's future mission vision.

When I arrived at Hyde Park Mennonite to interview with the search committee, all that remained of the former church plant group was a seventy-five-year-old historic building and fewer than twenty people, six of whom were voluntary service workers on a short-term mission assignment. No regular Sunday worship services were held, although a mid-week Bible study group met under the guidance of a retired pastor from First Church. Few of the current Bible study attendees had been part of the previous conflict. Fortunately for me as a new pastor, the "mother church" had relinquished its management role, and an extended time had lapsed between the end of the former church plant effort and this new one. What remained was a conviction that the church should be a vital part of its local community and that it should take a stand for peace with justice.

The birth narrative of a congregation and its subsequent history is important to understand. When a pastoral candidate reads the congregational profile and interviews various leaders, the congregation's efforts at introspection—or lack thereof—will become apparent. The candidate then needs to decide, along with those providing placement guidance, whether the congregation will be a good fit. If the congregation is still struggling with conflict issues, additional safeguards may need to be put in place prior to accepting the call. Denominational pastors can help make those decisions.

Under the definition of the denominational mission board, I was called a "church planter." This label meant the work was eligible for financial subsidy and significant regional oversight, which gave me confidence. However, this church plant also had a history that few attendees were fully aware of, but one that nevertheless continued to influence the mission of the congregation and my sense of a pastoral call. I inherited a small, socially active, community-based, politically involved congregation. Whenever a question like "Why is there a pool table in the basement?" was asked, the history would need retelling. The same history would be repeated when questions were asked about the level sanctuary floor or why folding chairs needed to be set up for Sunday worship each week.

As a way to honor the Hyde Park Mennonite's first leader—and to heighten my own awareness of the congregation's history—I began visiting him to express appreciation for his ministry at Hyde Park Mennonite. Even though he did not frequently attend worship, since he found it too painful, his family did participate in a home fellowship group before they eventually moved from the area. With a similar purpose, I met regularly for prayer and sharing with the new pastor at First Church. Eventually, he invited me to preach at First Church, and the breach between the two congregations began to heal.

Can God use a history that includes a fair amount of dysfunction and a young, inexperienced pastor for the building of God's kingdom? Of course! God was working for a long time to build my interest and compatibility with this congregation, so it was no coincidence that this small group and I were attracted to each other.

Even while in seminary, I was unknowingly preparing for this assignment. There, I was required to design a theoretical model of a congregation that could be supported through Scripture and historical example. A church plant would allow me to apply some of that learning.

Together, the congregation and I grew and matured in our faith, and we can testify with the Apostle Paul that we fought a good fight for the advancement of the gospel. I was a pastor in this congregation for fifteen years, and the church continues to flourish today.

6

The Weekly Sermon
—Deepening the Pastoral Call

Then Jesus said to the crowds and to his disciples, "The scribes and the Pharisees sit in Moses' seat; therefore, do whatever they teach you and follow it; but do not do as they do, for they do not practice what they teach."

—MATT 23:1–3

Journal Entry

Preaching is so time-consuming and difficult! Yet the radio preachers sound so confident and self-assured, sometimes even prideful. I wonder if they ever struggle with their sermons?

PREACHING IS A RIGOROUS undertaking of any solo pastorate. The weekly demand to produce a thought provoking, spiritually inspired, creative sermon is significant. People attend worship with a variety of expectations, and one is to hear good preaching. If a pastor doesn't feel inspired, too bad, because parishioners count on hearing a quality sermon—at least the majority of the time. The anticipation of a good sermon gives rise to my assertion that it is difficult to have meaningful pastor tenure without experiencing some success in proclamation. The connection of preaching to a pastoral vocation is a valid starting point for this discussion. The sermon remains a primary means for sharing the gospel and establishing a strong pastor/congregation bond. Preaching has commanded a sacred time slot in worship throughout the generations. Indeed, there have been far more alterations to music preferences and worship liturgy than to the preaching format. The time allotted for preaching in most worship services has perhaps been reduced, but its centrality remains, at least for the time being. The church's loyalty toward this sacred ritual seems unparalleled.

Because the sermon time is so visible and consistent in the life of the church, it becomes the most significant lens through which the congregation views its pastor. Week in and week out, members listen to their pastor. Often they are inspired, but other times, not so much. I don't know of another organization's leader, secular or faith-based, who is so public and consistently exposed to the stakeholder's introspection, critique, and evaluation.

In seminary homiletics classes, "good" preaching is evaluated according to the sermon's content, organization, relevancy, and actual delivery. These criteria remain significant for a pastor, but over the long haul, they become a bit less noteworthy. Another preaching standard that gains importance over time—so much so that it begins to rival the measures of a good sermon learned in homiletics class—is the pastor's lifestyle choices, habits, and behaviors. In other words, the pastor's congregation will likely ask, "Is the pastor living what's being preached?" or "Is there authenticity between the words and the actions of the pastor when witnessed in other settings?" Members want to see consistency between the message and the messenger.

Church members observe the pastor not only while preaching, but also in committee meetings, social events, and during crisis calls. If a pastor has a family, they too become a focus of congregational scrutiny. To be frank, many aspects of the pastor's life are put through the scrutiny of authenticity when parishioners listen to the weekly sermon. However, crippling fear of living in the proverbial "fishbowl" can hold a pastor hostage. The "fishbowl" is real, but the pastor has choices about how to live with this reality.

Consider this vignette: While assisting a small congregation with its pastoral review, a member told me that she has a hard time listening to her pastor on Sunday mornings. She went on to tell me about the time her pastor sat with her while she was in a hospital waiting room, nervously anticipating post-operative news from the doctor about her husband. She said the pastor talked incessantly on a variety of topics but never once inquired about the surgery or her own emotional state. She was visibly upset with her pastor and now tuned out his sermons. He had lost her confidence.

In another congregation, it became common knowledge that the pastor frequently lost his temper during the congregation's city league basketball games. The pastor's on-court behavior became a concern for some members and was mentioned later in a written pastoral review. The pastor seemed blindsided by this news, responding, "I don't understand. That's how I've always played basketball."

In yet another congregation, a senior member raised a question about the upcoming marriage of the pastor's adult child. As the story unfolded, I learned that the pastor's son was getting married to a divorced woman who had a child from her previous marriage. "I'm concerned about the example being set for our young people," stated the senior member.

The above illustrations, thankfully, reflect the perceptions of only a few. Most congregants are wonderfully forgiving and compassionately understanding of their pastor. For example, a minister going through a separation from his wife found the congregation standing with them both, even granting the pastor a paid leave during the height of the crisis. Another minister had to work through the reality of a spouse claiming to be homosexual, which ended the marriage. The congregation loved them both and gave the pastor time off to work through the shock and pain.

Preaching offers the pastor an opportunity, if she takes it, to integrate her life story in healthy ways, including its challenges and joys. The congregation has choices too in how they respond to their pastor's vulnerabilities—although some responses can be more hurtful than helpful.

The idea that public proclamation and lifestyle are interwoven is not a contemporary phenomenon. Remember when Jesus called the Pharisees hypocrites? "But woe to you, scribes and Pharisees, hypocrites! For you lock people out of the kingdom of heaven" (Matt 23:13). In today's vernacular, Jesus might be accusing them of being inauthentic. Jesus was issuing a warning to his disciples and followers: Beware when you see incongruity between the message and the messenger. The Pharisees had authority because they had the title and training to teach the Hebrew Scriptures, but they were not living the message. Earlier, in the Gospel of Matthew, Jesus was a bit softer in his indictment, but his point was the same. He accuses the teachers of the law: "for they do not practice what they teach" (Matt 23:3). Reading Jesus' words gives the impression that integrity between the spoken Word and the Word lived had paramount importance. Jesus might have said, "Don't tell people to live by the Law when you do not live by the same expectations." He could have also told the Pharisees, "If you have a hard time living the law, at least own up to the challenges, and say as much."

The Apostle Paul also highlighted this "practice what you preach" theme: "And I came to you in weakness and in fear and in much trembling. My speech and my proclamation were not with plausible words of wisdom" (1 Cor 2:3–4). Paul goes to great lengths to remind readers that his preaching ministry arises out of his connection to the people and not his eloquence. He uses the metaphor of the "clay jar" to illustrate how his preaching arises from his fragile human condition, not out of his training as a scholar: "But we have this treasure in clay jars, so that it may be made clear that this extraordinary power belongs to God and does not come from us" (2 Cor 4:7). His goal seems in direct opposition to that of his Pharisee colleagues. Paul made the point that he is preaching from a position of human weakness and frailty, not using the Pharisee title to gain advantage. On a side note, he did use his title when it served his advantage in a religious political controversy, saying, "Brothers, I am a Pharisee, a son of Pharisees" (Acts 23:6).

Make no mistake: the Apostle Paul was a scholar. Acts says, "I am a Jew, born in Tarsus in Cilicia, but brought up in this city at the feet of Gamaliel, educated strictly according to our ancestral law" (Acts 22:3). One gets the impression that Paul's educational vita is top notch and that he was conscious of when and where to use it. For instance, his training was used to engage other religious sects: "And Paul went in, as was his custom, and on three Sabbath days argued with them from the Scriptures" (Acts 17:2). As with Paul, there is a time and place for the use of a pastor's title and educational background, but in weekly sermons, a spirit of humility and an acknowledgment of struggles usually speaks louder. The key is to be aware of the audience and the purpose for disclosing one's educational background, training, or preaching experiences.

Over time, a few personal worship preparation disciplines emerged that made preaching easier and provided me with confidence. First, developing a long-range schedule of sermon topics and texts gave me the peace of mind that came of knowing my congregation was getting a balanced diet of preaching. Second, meeting regularly with the worship committee helped in planning services, including the use of creative media and music. Third, reading the Bible texts early in the week imbedded them in my mind and heart so they could ferment. Fourth, referencing commentaries and consulting my illustrations files provided me with useful background material. Fifth, reviewing preaching themes, as suggested by denominational worship resources and the *Revised Common Lectionary*, gave my preaching continuity and provided a theological skeleton from which to begin constructing my sermons. Sixth, staying alert to what was happening in the congregation and in the news provided ideas for later sermons. Seventh, writing daily in my journal was helpful in tracking prayers and tracing my ongoing conversations with God. While there is a glut of both written and electronic preaching resources available to the pastor, there is no substitute for prayer, study, and creativity when preparing and delivering the sermon.

My current pastor frequently uses historical religious artwork to illustrate his sermons. For instance, on Trinity Sunday he used artistic renditions of the Trinity to demonstrate how this difficult construct has evolved over time. As a result, I have a better understanding of an important cornerstone of Christian theology.

No amount of preparation and planning took away my nervousness related to preaching. I usually wrestled with some degree of self-doubt beforehand, asking myself, "Will my sermon inspire the congregation? Will my sermon make a difference in people's lives? Will the illustrations connect to the people and to the text? Will the Holy Spirit break through in the preparation and provide the encouragement or motivation that's needed?" Questions like these circled through my mind like a merry-go-round each week.

Managing anxiety around preaching has always been a challenge. I am not exaggerating when I claim that I have spent numerous sleepless nights fretting about Sunday's sermon. Thus, my preaching career began much like my teaching career in the public school—with apprehension! Sunday morning anxiety became evident in ice-cold hands. These freezing hands would betray an easy-going, friendly, and happy outward demeanor. Greeting parishioners Sunday morning was a bit embarrassing. After all, who wants to shake a pastor's cold hands? I soon realized that dunking my hands in warm water before mingling with members before the service started did not help, so I took to simply apologizing for my frigid hands. When the sermon was over, my hands would warm to a pleasant temperature as I became a confident pastor once again.

The cold hand malady served as a reminder of my special privilege of sharing the gospel message. Speaking to the gathered community about the good news of Jesus Christ, including Scriptural insights gleaned from study and prayer, was an honor I never took for granted. If my cold hands are ever warm prior to preaching, it may be a sign to find a new reminder.

Affirmation of preaching gifts from congregants can be a significant way to validate a pastor's call to ministry. However, feedback—whether positive or negative—can be somewhat misleading, as opinions on what constitutes a good sermon are extremely diverse. What one person appreciates, another finds mediocre. A sermon labeled "too scholarly" by one will be called "intellectually stimulating" by another. A pastoral friend told me he could accurately predict one member's affirmation of his sermon by how frequently he referenced his preaching notes: "The fewer times I looked down, the more affirmation he gave me for preaching a good sermon." Blending relevant subject matter with an engaging speaking methodology takes a great deal of effort, yet still doesn't ensure that all the varied interests of listeners will be met.

Member behavior, both verbal and non-verbal, can either help the pastor become more effective or detract from his confidence. For example, I preached in one congregation where a senior member sat in the back row clipping his fingernails. I later learned he had been performing this weekly Sunday ritual for years. The regulars seemed to tune out the annoying clipping sound, but not me, the guest preacher. In another congregation, a lay leader sitting in the second row read her Bible during the sermon, never making eye contact. When the pastor asked her why she read the Bible during the sermon, she responded, "It's difficult to listen when you use notes instead of relying on the Holy Spirit." This comment was a stinging blow to the pastor's self-confidence. Another church member consistently slept during the sermon. After a year or so of taking a snooze, he admitted his embarrassment. He assured the pastor it was not the preaching that put him to sleep but rather his farming lifestyle. He came to church exhausted after a busy week, and "the warmth of the building and relaxing atmosphere puts me to sleep. It's not a good habit," he confessed.

Preaching to the same congregation, week in and week out, is a privilege and honor, but it can also be an emotional roller coaster.

What inspires congregants one Sunday may not the next. Likewise, the pastor can have an off week. I recall an incident when, after numerous attempts to write a satisfactory sermon, I gave up just prior to worship. During the preaching portion of worship, I pulled up a chair and sat down in the front of the pulpit to tell the congregation of my dilemma. I recited all the different sermon tracks I had considered during the week to no avail, explaining that there was no sermon to give. After this short confessional, I paused and asked, "Can any of you identify with spiritual dry spells or a lack of creativity?" To my surprise, that question stimulated a wonderful exchange with many congregants. The conversation lasted through several of the weeks that followed. Some members left messages on the office phone, while others sent notes of affirmation to tell me their stories of struggle.

After the "non-sermon Sunday," the worship committee and I thought it would be beneficial to make regular space in services for members to interact with the sermon. Thus began a new ritual. My script after each sermon went something like this: "Now is the time for anyone to ask a question, affirm a point made, or share how God might be speaking to you. If there is silence, that's OK too; we will allow the Holy Spirit to speak to us in silence." I clarified that this was not a time for discussion but rather a moment to listen and share what God might be saying to us. Not infrequently, someone made a comment that deserved spontaneous prayer, and I asked those sitting closest to that individual to lightly lay their hands on her while we prayed. For those uncomfortable speaking in public (and there were many) the worship planners provided cards printed with a portion of Heb 10:25 that read, "Encouraging one another." These cards, collected along with the offering, provided valuable feedback from those who did not share publicly. These notes also became a way to connect pastorally to people expressing a need.

Sermon preparation time is extensive for pastors who believe their ministry of proclamation will make a difference in the world. My average sermon preparation time was ten to fifteen hours a week, which did not include the jotting of notes after a bicycle ride or reading. Neither does this time estimate include daily journal writing and prayer time. Weekly sermon preparation was a spiritual discipline that shaped my pastoral identity and created a bond with the congregation like no other ministry task. The writing, journaling, praying, reading, and connections these practices allowed me to draw between the Bible and the world deepened my biblical knowledge and strengthened my personal convictions. Likewise, the sermon delivery often led to powerful spiritual conversations with church members. Hearing a congregant respond to a sermon by claiming a new insight or deciding to change destructive behavior was inspiring.

Mystical, awe-inspiring moments sometimes occurred while writing sermons. One such experience illustrates this point, but first, a bit of background: My wife's Grandpa Lester, though not a pastor, read Bible commentaries the way most people read novels. When he passed away, I was the beneficiary of those commentaries and used them extensively in sermon preparation. During one particularly challenging moment of sermon preparation, a handwritten note in a margin of his book caught my attention. As I read, I began to well up with tears. Grandpa Lester's reflections on my problematic preaching text confirmed my then-tentative insights. I felt connected to Grandpa Lester, despite his death. I heard him speak to me through the scribbled note he had written years earlier: "You are on solid ground, keep going." I assume every pastor can give testimony to the mystery surrounding sermon preparation. When done sincerely, with ample time for prayer and study, God breaks through with a new awareness or insight that is exciting to share with the congregation.

For me, preaching connected the dots between the biblical text, study, prayer, life experiences, social and global realities, congregational life, and discernment. Preaching enhanced my call to pastoral ministry in a way few other aspects of ministry could. One antidote for pastors who have a difficult time with preaching: Name the deficiency, be honest with your limitations, ask for feedback, and continue to search for opportunities to improve.

7

Congregational Care
—Creating Trust

I am the good shepherd. I know my own and my own know me, just as the Father knows me and I know the Father; and I lay down my life for the sheep.

—JOHN 10:14–15

Journal Entry

Part of my job is providing "pastoral visitation." What exactly does pastoral care look like in an urban church when many in the congregation are employed during the day and most members are my age?

MOST JOB DESCRIPTIONS IDENTIFY pastoral care as an important part of a pastor's work, and it has to do with making personal connections in the congregation. Emotional bonding between members and pastor is crucial to meaningful long-term pastorates, and pastoral care helps that happen. When I consulted with one congregation, its members spoke with a unified voice when describing the kind of pastor they wanted next: "We want a pastor who will identify with us. We want a pastor who enjoys living and serving among us." They perceived their former pastor as emotionally disconnected and relationally difficult.

Pastors striving for excellence learn to know congregants and take a genuine interest in their lives. This reality is especially true for small-to-medium-sized congregations. Pastors who concentrate on only one aspect of pastoral work—preaching, for example—at the expense of providing pastoral care will miss valuable ministry opportunities. When members feel connected to their pastor, the pro bono benefit will be a confirmation and reaffirmation of a pastor's call into ministry. The foundation of this call is strengthened and enriched as pastors walk with people in their daily, weekly, and monthly life routines.

We need look no further than the example set by Jesus to see the importance of pastoral care. The sheer amount of space in the gospels dedicated to Jesus making personal, intimate connections with people is overwhelming. John 10:11–14 would be the most obvious place to read about Jesus' identity as a relational pastor. Here, in one of John's seven "I am" statements, Jesus identifies himself as the good shepherd—this metaphor being a job description of sorts. Jesus saw his calling from God, his vocation, as caring for people in the same way a shepherd might care for his sheep. In John 21:15–17, Jesus challenges his followers to "tend my lambs," and "shepherd my sheep."

Later, the apostles picked up on this shepherd language to describe their role in the new congregations popping up around the Mediterranean. Like Jesus, Apostle Peter identified the shepherd metaphor as a role for congregational leaders: "I exhort the elders among you to tend the flock of God that is in your charge" (1 Pet 5:1–2).

The Apostle Paul does not use the shepherd metaphor to describe his vocational calling, but he does use language that shows a similar intent. While exhorting the Ephesians, he writes, "You yourselves know how I lived among you the entire time from the first day that I set foot in Asia, serving the Lord with all humility and with tears, enduring the trials that came to me through the plots of the Jews" (Acts 20:18–19). One can easily imagine the shepherd-like intimacy that Paul developed with these new congregations. He was, in fact, quite zealous about their spiritual health and physical wellbeing.

The shepherd metaphor has carried over to modern times. Pastors are frequently referred to as "shepherds," even though the agrarian lifestyle described in Scripture seems far removed from our daily reality, particularly for those of us who live highly urbanized lives. The power of the metaphor, however, lies in its intent, not its literal interpretation. Jesus' illustrative exchanges with people, both in parable and reality, set the bar high for pastoral care ministry. The biblical image of a shepherd seems to be an unparalleled illustration of how to relate to those who have value and worth.

Pastors who engage with people—both in the church and in the broader community—find their ministry enriched and their call enhanced. Pastors who prioritize other areas of pastoral ministry at the expense of building relationships with parishioners lack the breadth and depth that so richly defined the ministries of Jesus and the Apostle Paul. Pastoral care happens any time a pastor meaningfully connects with people and is a natural outgrowth of ministry.

Stopping by a congregant's house, apartment, or long-term care facility for the specific purpose of reading the Bible, offering a prayer, or discussing matters of faith is one approach to pastoral visitation. However, methods of providing pastoral care can be much broader. Ministry can happen during a hallway conversation after a committee meeting or during a strategically placed phone call. Sending a text or email expressing interest in the other person's life is another way of connecting. Pastoral care can also happen during a recreational outing. For instance, a pastor might call a member who is an avid outdoorsman and suggest a fishing expedition. Pastoral care is also paying a hospital visit prior to a medical procedure or during recovery, or stopping by a new parent's house after childbirth and praying for the baby and it parents. Pastoral care is visiting a family in crisis due to any number of circumstances, including a member's sudden and unexpected death. It is answering the phone any time of the day or night and hearing the words, "Pastor, my mom just passed away. Can we talk?" Pastoral care means being available, interested, and willing to be an agent of God's grace in a variety of life situations. Good pastoral care also means being familiar with community resources for referral purposes.

One key word associated with pastoral care is "intentionality" because it translates to having a plan for connecting with all the members of a congregation. Without a system to track where and with whom the pastor is spending time, some people may not get a pastor's attention. I took brief notes about each of my encounters and kept these reminders in a secure spot. They were brief, but they included the date of the conversation and any subject matter that stood out. I reviewed the notes on a regular basis, and doing so always reminded me to pray for specific needs. If there were intervals longer than a couple of months between entries for a particular person, the gap would trigger a mental note to look for ways to engage them in conversation. These memos also became a memory jog to pick up a conversation topic from a prior visit. For example, to a member who had not been to worship for a lengthy period, I might have said, "John, I've missed seeing you. Are you still taking piano lessons, by the way?"

Intentionality also means clarifying expectations with members. Making assumptions about their pastoral care needs can be problematic. Members who feel slighted or taken for granted will sometimes express criticism of their pastor for not visiting them. More than once I've seen the surprised look on a pastor's face when confronted with a member's critique over a lack of pastoral attention. "I didn't think this family wanted me to visit. They always seem so busy and are already quite involved in the life of the church," came one surprised response from an unsuspecting pastor. A simple question could have helped this pastor clarify the member's expectations: "I like to stay connected with all our members. What is your preferred way for me to keep in touch, and with what frequency?

Setting relationship priorities is another indication of intentionality on the part of the pastor. One goal, for example, should be to stay connected with each congregant in some way. The temptation exists to associate only with those people who are most similar to us in their worldview, theology, interests, or life stage. In addition, every congregation has individuals who can easily dominate pastoral care time, often at the expense of the many hardworking and emotionally stable members. While the majority of congregants are happy to see their pastor attending to those needing special attention, pastors miss the opportunity to be rejuvenated by their more mature members when they don't allow time to interact with them as well.

Another group that needs pastoral attention are those on the edges of the faith community, those most different from the majority. These marginalized people can expand a pastor's perspective of God and the church. Scripture frequently—and with passion—addresses those that life has not treated well or relegated to the periphery. Listen to Ps 146:9, "The Lord watches over the strangers, he upholds the widow and the orphan." The words in Deut 10:19 remind the reader, "You shall also love the stranger." Jesus prioritized the "least of these" in his ministry. In Matt 25:45, he says, "Truly I tell you, just as you did not do it to one of the least of these, you did not do it to me."

One way I tried to expand my exposure to the vulnerable or marginalized such as those referred to in the biblical texts was by knocking on doors in the immediate neighborhood to introduce myself. Many of those neighborhood connections turned out to be senior citizens. These new relationships provided a wonderful break from normal routines, and they eventually evolved into a significant ministry. I became a pastor to them and was frequently introduced to their families. When a senior was forced to move from living independently to a care facility, I listened to confessions of guilt from their adult children. I also witnessed another senior's anger, aimed at his children and at God, when forced to give up the car keys. Time spent listening and reflecting back what I heard, often offering to pray, was part of my sacred ministry of pastoral care.

However, lest readers think I took these visits too seriously, I need to confess that on more than one occasion I entered the warm confines of a senior's home and promptly got sleepy. In one instance when I caught myself nodding off while listening to the third version of the same story, I asked Phoebe if she would mind if I took a quick five-minute catnap on the recliner chair I was sitting in. She responded as though I had given her a great compliment: "Oh, you are just like one of my kids. That's what they do." When I heard that, I knew we had made a connection.

In contrast to visiting this senior's home, I seldom made a pastoral visit to the homes of congregants who were not elderly or in crisis. I felt more comfortable meeting for breakfasts, lunches, or coffee—particularly with men in the congregation. I also visited members in their work places. Sometimes I prayed with people, many times I did not. During one hike with a congregant and his friends, we stopped and looked at the majestic view, and I asked, "Do you mind if I pray for us at this spot?" At that moment, during a spontaneous prayer, pastoral care happened.

I had a more difficult time finding appropriate ways to provide pastoral care with women my age. When I began my pastoral career, there seemed to be an epidemic of sexual misconduct cases on the part of pastors making regular appearances on the nightly news. The reputation of pastors plummeted. As a way of combating this negative pastoral image, I often invited female members to visit with me at the church. The office felt more appropriate than meeting at a restaurant. However, I later learned that pastor's offices were frequently the location of choice for pastoral misconduct.

Anxiety around sexual misconduct peaked midway through my pastoral tenure when a young single woman confessed to having sexual dreams about me. I was in shock! She went on to tell me that her mental health therapist suggested she talk with me about her fantasies. Uncertain as to how to respond to her at the time, I told her I needed some time to think about it. I waited a few days, prayed intensely, and discussed the matter with my wife. She counseled me to tell this parishioner that I was happily married and that it wasn't appropriate or comfortable for me to listen to her fantasies. Instead, she should go back to her therapist to discuss them. My emotional load was lifted, the parishioner accepted my response, and fortunately the topic never resurfaced.

As a result of my personal insecurity in knowing how to provide pastoral care to women, Rebecca and I did a lot of entertaining in our home. She was a true co-pastor, and she participated fully in making hospitality an intentional part of building relationships. More than once we pored over the church phone list to help us review members to invite next. Hospitality was a powerful means of building rapport and creating bonds, but it was also exhausting.

As the congregation grew, it became impossible to provide pastoral care with the same intensity. Following a conversation with congregational leaders, a Congregational Care Committee (CCC) was formed. Criteria were developed and members with the applicable gifts were invited to serve. Together, the CCC and I prioritized their pastoral care work as three-fold: calling on first-time visitors, contacting those missing from worship for an extended period, and visiting ill or rehabilitating members at home. Through monthly meetings, the CCC became a wonderful partnership between pastor and gifted laypersons all working together to provide pastoral care.

When a congregant included our family as guests at a party or a social gathering, Rebecca and I were quick to accept. Those occasions exposed us to non-church-going people as an opportunity to develop new friendships. At one particularly memorable event, we and the other guests assembled in the basement family room to view photographs of the host's recent expedition to Yosemite. While climbing the stairs to the main floor after the presentation, I reached up to squeeze my wife's behind, certain that no one else would notice in the packed stairway. The horrifying news was that my hand found the wrong posterior, and I inadvertently pinched another woman. Startled, she jumped, turned around, and glared at me as if I was one of the aforementioned sexual predator pastors. Of course, I apologized profusely, right there on the stairway. Fortunately, two factors were in my favor: My victim had a sense of humor, and Rebecca began laughing so hard she had tears. Before long, the entire group had heard the story, and I became a true "butt" of pastoral jokes.

Incidents like this one created long-term memories, as did many other pastoral care moments. The longer I remained at one congregation, the deeper the pastoral relationships became, many evolving into personal friendships. Thus, the line between friendship and pastoral care became blurred at times. I was not aware of how confusing my pastoral role could be, however, until the following situation came to light many months later: A congregant, also a good friend, was experiencing marital difficulties. During this crisis, I reached out in support, but he did not know how to receive my overtures. Confused, he wondered whether I had visited him as a friend or as his pastor. He later confessed his confusion and the fact that he wanted me to relate to him as a pastoral counselor rather than as his friend. I was surprised and hurt, not realizing I should have spelled out my role upon reaching out.

A related story further illustrates this confusion: A pastor attended a high school basketball game in a neighboring town and referenced the trip in his pastoral care report at a church council meeting. A council member took issue and questioned why mention of the trip was made in the pastoral report. "Attending a basketball game doesn't seem like a pastoral requirement," he stated. What the councilperson didn't know was that one of the congregation's high school basketball players was having some challenges at school, and the pastor thought attending his game would help build trust and rapport. This pastor later reported to me that he rode to and from the ballgame with a member of the congregation who told him stories of his marital stress, and at the game he sat next to another parishioner who confided in him about his work-related stress.

A dilemma for this pastor—and many pastors—relates to transparency about the use of pastoral care time. Few truly understand the complexities of a pastor's role. Fewer still comprehend the realities of family dysfunction, spiritual challenges, and psychological problems that fellow parishioners bring to the congregation, and because of confidentiality guidelines, pastors cannot freely share many of their interactions.

A pastor friend told me of being physically attacked and choked by a parishioner in the privacy of the parishioner's home. The pastor was afraid for his life. Afterwards, when the pastor told a congregational leader about the attack, the response he heard was, "You must have caught Brad on a bad day," and then he laughed. Extreme example? Maybe, but it demonstrates how congregants can have a difficult time comprehending the seriousness of the misbehavior and wrongdoing on the part of some fellow parishioners.

The multiplicity of roles—pastor, confidant, counselor, and friend—means a pastor needs to compartmentalize at times. Pastors often know more intimate details about parishioners than they may care to know. A member being accused of infidelity by his spouse might also be the chairperson of the building and grounds committee. This same member might attend a social event that includes the pastor. From my experience, it is best for a pastor to have self-imposed amnesia—pretending not to know anything other than what's happening at the moment. Of course, there are always exceptions, as in the case of trust violations or the breaking of laws.

What about pastoral care for pastors? Pastors do well to consider carefully how and where they will get their support in difficult times. For instance, is it ever appropriate for a pastor to share their marital or family challenges, or even major theological questions, from the pulpit or to people in the congregation? While there are no specific guidelines that I'm aware of, careful attention should be given to where and with whom a pastor self-discloses. One pastor confessed from the pulpit his addiction to pornography and asked for prayer. His decision to share publicly a private addiction was highly inappropriate and should have been addressed with his bishop, district pastor, or therapist. Speaking personally, I never discussed marriage stress or sexual issues with the congregation. My sermons told parishioners enough of my spiritual journey and life specifics. To do more intimate sharing felt voyeuristic. I believe maintaining a level of professionalism, including setting appropriate limits on self-disclosure, is critical to a pastor's success.

Pastors need outlets outside the congregation for working through personal concerns. But pastors also need a safe cluster of individuals within the congregation to discuss personal or family issues that have the potential to impede their work or effectiveness. One option that works well is a pastoral care group or committee. With this arrangement, pastors carefully select a few mature and respected members to serve in the group, formed specifically for pastor-initiated topics. With good boundaries and a common understanding of roles, a pastor can be assured of confidentiality, wisdom, and prayer.

Pastors in relationship with congregants become the agents of grace, the dispensers of grounded counsel, the voice of reason, and a healing touch. Pastors who know their role as shepherds feel the tug of God on their vocational pursuits as they serve the church. When members feel nurtured and cared for by their pastor, they will reciprocate, resulting in confirmation of a pastor's sense of call.

8

Community Involvement
—Extending a Congregation's Influence

And the King will answer them, truly I tell you, just as you did to one of the least of these who are members of my family, you did to me.

—MATT 25:40

Journal Entry

Sometimes I feel schizophrenic, like I have two vocations. One is in the confines of the church building where I prepare sermons and have my office. The other is in the community and neighborhood. I wish these two worlds intersected more, as I really enjoy both.

THE CONGREGATION WAS SMALL, fewer than twenty attendees at first. I was salaried part-time through a combination of funding sources that included the congregational offerings, a conference subsidy, and a small "love offering" from my home congregation in Colorado. My wife also worked part-time as a Registered Nurse to help provide us a living wage.

Since my new ministry was a church plant, there were bylaws, constitution, policy, and budget work to be done in those early months—not a problem, since I had a propensity for administration! Sermon preparation and pastoral care were enjoyable tasks that also took time, but not enough to fill up my week. Plus, I hated sitting in the office each and every day. I found myself wanting more relational and intellectual stimulation. Bluntly speaking, I was bored! "Where would my new profession, my new calling, intersect with the community?" I wondered. That was the question I needed to resolve. I wanted to feel productive, like my time was well spent.

After a few ventures into the community, I found a wonderful assortment of interesting people with whom I developed lifelong friendships, and, in some cases, ministry opportunities. I learned that pastoral ministry can be profound beyond measure when non-churchgoers meet a pastor they can relate to. I also discovered the wonderful grace and mystery of God, who resides both within and beyond the confines of a church building. I can say without hesitation that community involvement did more to augment my pastoral identity than any other dimension of ministry.

I began this foray into the community by attending the local ministerial association—two of them, to be exact. One was the Evangelical Ministerial Association, and the other was the Ministerial Alliance made up of the mainline denominations. In these organizations, I formed peer relationships and a few lasting friends. I learned about other denominational politics and belief, and they learned about Mennonites. I learned that suspicion, animosity, distrust, and downright hostility across the theological divide ran wide and deep. However, the interfaith peer connections I made were important, in part, because I had elicited trust and confidence.

Enrolling in a Clinical Pastoral Education (CPE) program at the local hospital gave me an opportunity to think critically and purposefully about pastoral care ministry. As part of the CPE program, I was required to volunteer as a chaplain at a large city hospital, where I learned firsthand the value of pastoral care to the dying and critically wounded.

While deep into sermon preparation on a quiet weekday morning, my hospital beeper summoned me to the emergency room. There I found distressed staff; one of their own, a nurse's son, had been shot. As the story leaked out, I learned the boy's father had shot his son through a locked bathroom door in fit of rage. Crisis ministry became real that day.

In CPE, I met a modern-day saint, Richard, who became a close friend and confidant. He had been a parish priest for fourteen years and then married his friend, a Catholic nun. Together they had one son who was the same age as mine. Their decision to marry left Richard without a parish, so he needed to discover a new vocation; he was retooling to become a chaplain. Drawing on his passion for the aged, he asked me to help him form a nonprofit called Ministry to the Aged, which I served for ten years as a member of the board of directors. This organization provided chaplaincy services to long-term care facilities in need. Money gathered from local churches supported Richard in his role as ecumenical chaplain to some of the neediest members of society. Many of the people Ministry to the Aged served had belonged to a faith community at one time, but those communities had long forgotten them.

By joining a local peace and justice organization, I found many like-minded people who shared similar views on the political issues of the day. However, few from this group drew from the teachings of Christ as their foundation for political action. Although I was often the only pastor present at meetings, I gained confidence in expressing a point of view that reflected Christ's words. Thus, in this peace and justice sector of the community, my prophetic voice became strong, and respect for our small congregation grew.

National issues related to war captured local interest and spawned public protests. Along with other members of the congregation, I participated in many demonstrations, including one protesting the shipment of nuclear waste through the state on the way to treatment plants. On one cold December night, fifty protesters, many from our local fellowship, gathered in support of those who were performing acts of civil disobedience. I was asked to speak and pray—a common assignment at these gatherings.

Involvement with other social activists became central to my pastoral ministry and identity. I stepped into a community void of a voice expressing Christ's message of peace and justice as a central component of the gospel message. Eventually, a few Christians and I from the social activist community felt called to begin the "Ecumenical Peace Fellowship" as a forum for Christians who needed a corporate voice and a safe place for conversation. A number of these folks, searching for a congregation home, eventually found one in the church where I pastored.

Being a historic peace church had its challenges too. For example, when Billy Graham came to the city, I felt tremendous pressure from some church members and the Evangelical Ministerial Association to recruit counselors and help promote this ecumenical evangelism effort. However, I knew that Graham was refusing to endorse an international nuclear disarmament initiative and, like others in our Ecumenical Peace Fellowship, thought he should be promoting a gospel that included a stronger peace emphasis. In response, a few area pastors and many congregants from a variety of churches handed out flyers in the parking lot to those attending the crusade. The flyer proclaimed the dangers of the nuclear arms race and quoted the words of Jesus, who taught us to love our enemies in Matt 5:43–48. Our actions caught the eye of the local newspaper, and conversations began, though they were not always friendly even among my local congregation.

Not infrequently, transients called the church office asking for groceries or money. Fortunately, the congregation provided a monthly allowance for this purpose. One of these men, Scott, I remember well. My mother would have called a man like Scott, a "poor soul." As I understood her term, "poor souls" were folks who could never quite get their lives together. What was interesting about Scott and many of these transient men was their knowledge of the Bible. Scott listened to Christian radio from morning to late afternoon. In the evenings, he went to a local bar. There, he often attracted women who took him home after he was too intoxicated to find his way back to a downtown hotel room, or wherever he was calling home at the time.

For a number of years, Scott became a regular fixture in my life. He'd leave town dreaming about the next job he was going to get, but he'd always end up back in town. Every time he returned, he called me to explain how his life was taking a turn for the better. Toward the end of the conversation, a request for bus money would come. "Once I get to Long Beach, I have a great job waiting, and I'll send you the money," he would add at the end of our chat.

One Christmas Eve, as our family and extended family gathered around the table, my adrenalin spiked when I received an urgent call from the local police department. As the story unfolded, they reported that a man with a gun named Scott was holed up in a house nearby, refusing to come out unless "his pastor" came to the home. I went, uncertain what I'd find. Sure enough, police were surrounding Scott's residence! As I peered through the front window, waiting for the police's signal, I saw empty beer bottles and a shotgun on the kitchen table next to Scott. Once inside, I found an inebriated Scott, lamenting his lot in life. After what seemed like an eternity, I convinced him to go with me to a detox center. (The police had given him the choice of either detox or jail.) This incident seemed to be the beginning of a journey toward a changed life for Scott. At last contact, I learned he had become a commercial bus driver.

Another intriguing character, Mark, to whom I had given gas money a few times, showed up at worship one Sunday. After the service he waited until most people had left the building, then asked if we could visit sometime. As his story unfolded, I learned he had a passion for "saving" Jews. He had made several trips to Israel and had even learned to speak Hebrew. While Mark never asked for money or attended worship services again, he did stop by the church office frequently to talk, mostly about God's plan for the Jews. I hadn't heard from him for a long time until one day, out of the blue, he called to ask if I would ride to a nearby city park with him, claiming he had a gift for me. My mind flashed to scenarios of Mark doing me harm, since I sometimes doubted his mental stability and we did have theological disagreements from time to time. I subdued those fears with a deep breath and prayer as we drove to the park and hiked to a hilltop overlooking the city. He brought out a box from his well-worn backpack. Inside, wrapped in tissue, was a stunningly beautiful Jewish prayer shawl, called a *tallit*. As I unfurled the white linen of the *tallit*, he spoke about the significance of our conversations to his faith journey and expressed gratitude for my acceptance of him. Mark's act of generosity touched me immensely, particularly since it came from someone I least expected.

This moment of grace reminded me of the story of the woman who anointed Jesus' feet with expensive perfume and then dried them with her hair. The story is one of only a few that gets the attention of all four gospel writers, and they capture it in amazing detail (Luke 7:36–50; John 12:1–6; Matt 6:6–13; Mark 14:3–9). The woman, called Mary by John and labeled a "sinner" by the other three, was clearly one of the "poor souls" Jesus prioritized in his ministry. The gifts Jesus gave were time, acceptance, and compassion. What he received was love and appreciation, demonstrated by Mary's extravagance.

There were many of these "poor souls" in my ministry. In hindsight, I can see more clearly how they were strong advocates for my ministry, and thus my pastoral call. They all wanted something, maybe a little gas or bus money, but mostly they wanted acceptance—to be recognized as having potential. Because the local congregation gave me the opportunity and time, these men became an important part of my ministry. Members of my congregation rarely became acquainted with them, except through a monthly pastoral report or when one happened to attend worship for a short period.

Cross-cultural ministry was another opportunity to affirm my calling as a pastor. A small Hispanic congregation in our denomination was emerging in a neighboring city about the time I began pastoring. This congregation's pastor and I became fast friends, frequently meeting for shared conversation and prayer. We exchanged pulpits on occasion, but more often I preached during Sunday evening service at his congregation while he translated. Through this friendship and our shared ministry, he taught me the importance of prayer and dependence on God. In our Anglo congregation, the default for solving a problem or meeting a need was raising money. In this Hispanic setting, where money was scarce and many members were transients, the default for any situation was impassioned prayer to seek God's wisdom and intervention.

Connecting the heart to the head with matters of spirituality was a challenge for me personally and for the highly educated, urban congregation where I pastored. For instance, many members wanted our worship and sermons to connect to environmental concerns. I suggested to the worship planning team that on Easter we take a sunrise walk in the local park and ask those who attend to pick up trash along the way. We would conclude the walk on top of a hill overlooking the city, where we would read Scripture, sing, and pray. The idea was embraced with enthusiasm, and the planning began.

Leaders handed out the trash bags as twenty attendees spread out across the park and crisscrossed to the top of the sagebrush-covered hill, gathering food wrappers, cigarette butts, diapers, an old tire, and discarded cans along the way. Overlooking the city at the end of the hike, we sang familiar Scripture songs. I led a brief meditation related to creation care and new life (2 Cor 5:17.) followed by a time of prayer. The city newspaper got wind of this "unusual tradition" and wrote an article. The next Easter the number of trash gatherers multiplied, and many stayed for a brunch afterwards at the church. Every opportunity to connect the gospel to the community seemed to yield new relationships. Some of these connections evolved into long-term faith commitments to the body of Christ.

The editorial section of the local newspaper kept me in touch with which city, state, national, and global events might have theological overtones. For instance, the death penalty topic appeared frequently in the local news, so I wrote an editorial column speaking about the sacredness of life and the gospel message. My son, a high school student at the time, said his social studies teacher was using the article as a classroom discussion starter.

One day, the state penitentiary chaplain called to ask if I would come visit a number of inmates who had expressed interest in our denomination. With eagerness, I arranged a visit, curious as to what God might be up to. I was escorted to a room where twenty new converts eagerly awaited my arrival. Following a few introductory comments, I quickly discovered the men were more interested in growing beards than in joining the Mennonite Church. (A rumor had circulated that being a Mennonite meant the warden would allow facial hair.) But, even with no new converts, this encounter led to a few enduring relationships, and for a number of years I made a monthly trip to the prison to lead a Bible study.

Community involvements became sermon fodder, providing practical illustrations and creating a natural agenda for leadership team meetings. One outgrowth of my citywide involvements was recognizing the need for more public meeting spaces. A policy was developed to open the church building, at little or no cost, to non-profit groups that aligned with the congregation's mission. Before long, an Alcoholic's Anonymous chapter, the local neighborhood association, a homebirth education group, and a music and dance group for children all used the facility. Meetings were advertised with our congregation's name listed as the meeting place—giving us great publicity.

The church began to grow, worship attendance increased. Fifteen soon became twenty-five, and later fifty, until there were often over one hundred people participating in worship.

Ecumenical and social involvements helped reflect a congruent identity—an identity centered on the congregation's vision statement: *A church seeking God's peace for the world. All seekers are welcome!* These words were printed on an outdoor sign near the entrance as a beacon for anyone interested in the gospel message. Not infrequently, a guest would point to the vision statement as their reason for attending a service.

Community ministry changed my pastoral identity, transforming the uncertainty and insecurities I had felt into bold confidence. My pastor title became a more comfortable fit, opening more doors for ministry than it closed. Just as importantly, the local congregation served as my "base of operation," my spiritual home, a safe place to deprogram. These connections built a foundation of conviction and belief that would withstand self-doubt and conflicts in the body of Christ that otherwise might have shaken my call.

9

Leadership
—Building Missional Communities

Give your servant [Solomon] therefore an understanding mind to govern your people, able to discern between good and evil; for who can govern this your great people? It pleased the Lord that Solomon had asked this.

—1 Kgs 3:9–10

Journal Entry

I worry about reoccurring headaches. Are they work-related? Rebecca thinks so. There are always loose ends that defy tying up. Seldom, if ever, do I feel a sense of accomplishment, like a job well done. Lord, help me to see your presence in the unresolved.

WARS SEEM TO DEFINE generations, often by the leadership styles that emerge afterward. For example, strong visionaries formed mission agencies, schools, and program boards after World War I and II under the auspices of various denominational institutions. The Korean War provided leaders who managed these institutions. They were loyal to the previous generation's vision of expansion. The Vietnam War created a generation of skeptical leaders—the baby boomers. They were, at least in their early years, ambivalent or even resistant to leading these same institutions. Loyalty was questioned, not assumed. More recently, the Gulf Wars and the wars in Afghanistan and Iraq have fashioned a collaborative, innovative leadership model. Current leaders seem less tied to historical institutions and more intent on looking for new alliances between and outside denominational boundaries.

My entry into pastoral ministry was highly influenced by the Vietnam War. Anyone in authority, pastors included, were suspect for being part of "the establishment." That phrase, "the establishment," was a catchall description depicting institutions ranging from corporations to congregations both large and small. This post-Vietnam War era of leaders was not as interested in the church of their parents, grandparents, and great-grandparents.

To call oneself Mennonite, Lutheran, Episcopalian, or Presbyterian has not been fashionable since the 1970s. From this time forward, independent, non-denominational church revitalization movements grew in popularity. New groups such as the Jesus People, Calvary Chapel, Vineyard Ministries, and a host of Charismatic offshoot congregations sprouted everywhere. If and when boomers were attracted to the church, they felt motivated by something other than denominational loyalty. Despite this suspicion toward denominations, however, there existed a high level of commitment to the local congregation. No longer could a pastor depend on denominational loyalty as a significant resource in building a congregation, especially in the urban areas. Rather, those seeking a church experience looked for a congregation that seemed like a good fit rather than a specific denomination, even if it meant breaking a long-standing family tradition. I attended seminary during this time of societal transition.

Today this migration away from specific denominations continues and is best exemplified by the prominence of mega-churches such as Saddleback, Mars Hill, and Willow Creek Community Church, to name only a few. Their influence on the local congregation cannot be underestimated. Often, these large congregations spin-off new pastors who begin to replicate the mother church in a new community. Similarly, the "emerging church movement" continues to signal more independence from a denominational identity. In these new congregations that emphasize independence from "organized religion" and historic denominational connections, there seems to be little evidence of authority existing apart from the local congregation's pastor.

This highly centralized approach to church management was vastly different from my understanding of leadership when I began pastoral ministry. At that time, not only were institutions suspect, so was leadership, including pastoral. As a result, I dropped the pastor title as sure as a snake sheds its skin. Instead, I referred to myself as a "facilitator." This title fit well with my recent seminary training, which emphasized the importance of servant leadership. Right or wrong, my understanding of this leadership model was more laissez-faire: let the group work out the details without pastoral influence. After all, I would probably leave after a few years, so this was their church more than mine. My job was to ask good questions and assist in creating an atmosphere where the community could speak with one another.

My approach to a facilitative kind of leadership was highly relational, and I avoided conflict at all costs. A good relationship with congregants trumped implementing a long-range strategy, especially if the plan would cause stress. The biblical image of leadership was the towel and basin, which I interpreted as empowering others but giving few suggestions for goal setting or defining tactics to meet the goals. My role was to preach good sermons and encourage people to get involved.

The evolution from this facilitative role took time—more than a few years. As a facilitator, I tried not to stand apart, offer many suggestions, or presume to have responsibility for outcomes.

I was simply one attendee among many attendees. As a facilitative leader, I assumed that all participants had a right to influence group decisions and that all voices were of equal quality. Business meetings and group discussions were long and exhausting. Finding conclusions to decisions ranging from whether to put indoor/outdoor carpet on the front steps to what Sunday school curriculum to purchase occupied an enormous amount of group decision-making time. We were all in this work together—at least that was what I kept telling myself.

Over time, this model of leading and decision-making did not work for some, myself included. There was a growing discontent with these time-intensive after-worship meetings. Holding opinions in check and fretting that being directive or assertive might squelch someone's spirit was taking an emotional toll, plus I felt disempowered. I mistakenly interpreted real leadership as being authoritative in nature.

One congregational decision illustrates this tension: A vacuum was needed, and a senior member (one of the very few who were over sixty) wanted to purchase a specific brand, a Rainbow. As the story emerged, I learned that this member had recently had a spiritual conversation with the vacuum salesman. Buying the vacuum might be a win-win went the argument from this member: the church would get a vacuum, and a new family might attend our congregation. The congregation labored over this decision with the same intensity as beginning a building project. Finally, out of frustration, the member who wanted the Rainbow donated half of the vacuum's cost. As it turned out, the salesman never darkened the church doorway, and for years afterward various volunteer janitors complained bitterly about the vacuum and started bringing their own from home.

As a facilitative pastor, I got "sucked in" to the laborious vacuum cleaner decision and wonder now how such a small decision carried such emotional weight! Our choice of vacuum seems miniscule when compared to later congregational tensions. However, at the time, the success or failure of my ministry rested on a resolution that kept everyone happy. My unwritten goal was to be well liked by the parishioners and stay neutral as I facilitated a group process. There was no place in my leadership vocabulary or methodology for directive leadership that allowed me to express my opinions.

Controversial topics seem never-ending when building God's kingdom. Of course, some will be more intense than others, but I can safely assert that most congregations, at any given time, will likely have a low-grade conflict brewing. Conflict is simply the nature of most organizations, and the church is no exception. What also seems true is that congregations spend a lot of time avoiding or minimizing conflict rather than developing strategies that use conflict as a tool for ministry. Scriptures are not shy in describing the tensions existing in the early church. Romans 14:1–7 highlights the relationship strain surrounding holy days and food. Acts 15 illustrates the conflict between Jews and Gentiles. First Corinthians 3 tells of the organizational anxiety surrounding church leadership. These texts, and many more, demonstrate that conflict was a normal part of early church life. I would hasten to add that Scripture is clear that although conflict is common within the faith community, it is not a goal; forgiveness, reconciliation, and unity are the hoped-for outcomes.

Ephesians 4:1–6 reminds us of our common "bond of peace" found through Jesus Christ and the Holy Spirit. Matthew 18:15–20 describes a specific method for resolving individual conflicts. Galatians 6:1–5 challenges the reader to have a gentle spirit and fair-minded attitude when relating to another who has fallen from grace. Second Corinthians 5:18 reminds every believer they have been given the "ministry of reconciliation." Yet congregations nearly always lack the policy and procedures to guide believers through disagreements.

There were plenty of congregational tensions in my ministry that helped shape my emerging leadership style. Some of those challenges included: criteria for membership versus a fluid membership, building remodel versus global missions, intentional church growth versus laissez-faire growth, and intimacy in worship versus formality in worship. I soon discovered that taking an active role in leadership felt more authentic and honest than maintaining a self-imposed neutrality.

A cathartic moment occurred for me at a national church convention where I attended a leadership workshop led by three African-American pastors. The presenters invited those of us in attendance to live up to our calling to lead Christ's church. They spoke with a confidence I only hoped to have. I noticed they were all wearing liturgical prayer stoles, an uncommon symbol in my religious tradition. After the service, I walked to the presenter podiums to give a word of affirmation to one of the speakers with whom I was personally acquainted. What prompted my next question I'll never know, but I asked rather directly, "Who gave you permission to wear a prayer stole?"

Without the least bit of hesitation, my friend took off his prayer stole and placed it over my shoulders. As he did so, he spoke these words: "I give you permission, Larry, to wear this stole. Go forth empowered to lead." I stood in front of my friend, initially in shock. Then, I thanked him profusely for his generosity, his confidence in God's church, and for our friendship. His prayer stole came to represent, for me, the role of pastor as a more centralized leader; it helped give balance to the towel and basin symbol I had singularly embraced. In the future these two symbols provided the needed equilibrium to my ongoing leadership style. Later, when I had judicatory responsibilities, I gave a prayer stole to every new pastor in our conference. The gift served two functions: To begin a conversation with congregational leaders about the role of pastoral leadership and to symbolize the importance of the pastoral office in each congregation.

Back in the local congregation, my newfound leadership confidence was tested. The church's involvement in peace and justice issues attracted new people, but at the same time it challenged members who thought the church should not be vocal in political matters. As tension crept in to conversations during worship planning and other meetings, I worked to keep credibility with the most evangelical part of our congregation while continuing to provide support to those writing letters to the editor and attending protest rallies. I was personally quite involved in public social witness and continued to be invited to speak out at public gatherings. My public stance caused further strain with a segment of the congregation who did not have the same political sensitivities and who held a different core view of the church's role in society. Those with contradictory views found my public media exposure disturbing. They did not like reading about their congregation, or its pastor, in the newspaper.

Keeping in regular conversation with those who held differing ideas through phone calls, coffees, and lunches seemed important. These discussions were respectful but didn't necessarily end with a change of opinion. However, these links did develop trust and build confidence in the pastor/congregant relationship. I learned that when fervently held convictions are combined with honesty and self-reflection between pastor and congregant, there is hope for maintaining the relationship long-term. Most people seemed to respond positively to compassionate and open conversation. They did not abandon our relationship or the church because of a difference of opinion or a variant conviction alone.

I asked the most oppositional members how our congregation's peace witness was personally affecting them. Why were they upset? What could I learn? The discovery was fascinating and enlightening. Some members were embarrassed to bring guests to worship, especially if the guest might be of a more conservative political persuasion. Worship had a political flavor that was a deterrent to a welcoming congregation. Additionally, they felt that public statements and newspaper publicity gave the impression that everyone in the congregation had the same political perspective. These less politically-minded members felt isolated by the tone of many in the peace activist sector of the church. Somehow, the peace activism translated to a related complaint that the informal dress in worship had become a stumbling block. As one person described worship, "There is no respect for being in the presence of God."

In response, I tried not to use the sermon time as a place to argue a point of view. I spoke of personal convictions and tried to intersect personal faith and social issues with Jesus' teachings and the entire Bible. I tried to be self-disclosing about personal biases and struggles, rather than acting as if I had the final, authoritative word. It was during this period that I began leaving time after each sermon for a word of affirmation, a new insight, or a question the sermon had stimulated. I started, on occasion, wearing a coat and tie in worship as a way to visibly demonstrate that I had heard the informality concerns. Modeling change could originate with the pastor.

A change in attitudes between the peace activists and the evangelical portion of the congregation happened slowly as community members were attracted to the church, many because of its public peace witness. Those frustrated with the peace emphasis found a new commonality in evangelism. The new attendees lowered the tension. The seekers found the Mennonite peace message attractive, and this numeric growth became a shared value between the peace witness advocates and the evangelistic witness contingent. I discovered through this experience that people would not automatically leave the congregation because of contrary opinions.

Eventually, the initial excitement of more people attending worship wore off. The new reality was that congregational life was not the same as it had been. The familiar intimacy in worship was getting lost, and a variety of voices lamented this fact: "I don't know everyone in the congregation anymore," "It's just isn't like it used to be," or "I don't feel comfortable sharing in the larger group."

In order to meet members' fellowship needs and help them mature in their discipleship and faithfulness to Christ, the congregational leadership team, of which I was a part, initiated "small groups." Joining small groups was voluntary but seriously promoted. The outcome was that a large percentage of the congregation starting meeting together in groups of six to ten once a week or every other week, usually in homes. The leadership team provided the necessary structure and format for the groups. The biblical backdrop to this initiative was Acts 2:42: "They devoted themselves to the apostles' teaching and fellowship, to the breaking of bread and the prayers."

The increased numbers created organizational stress and anxiety, and I was unsure how to guide the congregation through this growth phase. However, a leadership grace moment occurred when our congregation was selected for a strategic planning grant by the denomination in partnership with the Lilly Foundation. A consultant was assigned to assist our congregation with clarifying its vision. One full year of intense work finally resulted in commonly agreed-upon goals related to church growth, including plans for accommodating the increased numbers. A side benefit of this project was the confidence I gained in working alongside the advisor. The consultant, who also was a pastor, helped to manage anxiety—both the congregation's and my own. He was God's answer to my prayers of uncertainty.

My leadership style continued to shift from the neutral facilitator who tried to keep the peace at all costs to a pastor leader who provided options, expressed opinions, and kept people talking. This more directive model meant a larger pastoral investment in the congregation's spiritual and organizational health. I began asking more strategic questions, such as: Where is God calling us? What ideas do congregational leaders have for moving the congregation forward? Where do our ideas converge in a common vision? Who are the people that can help us reach this goal? As congregants saw evidence of my pastoral leadership, plus a strong commitment to building a vibrant faith community, the congregation-to-pastor relationship deepened. Whether imagined or real, I seemed to garner a growing respect. Just as importantly, I began to trust even more that the call of God to be pastor was real.

The prayer of King Solomon was a near daily mantra throughout my ministry: "Give me an understanding mind to govern your people" (1 Kgs 3:9). During active pastoral ministry, I repeated this verse so often it became second nature to think of Solomon prior to any meeting. One insight that came after reading this passage in its larger context was "I always have a choice how to respond." Solomon gave me permission to be inventive rather than bound to the expected response. There always seems to be a choice, even if the options are limited. The "understanding mind" of Solomon was pliable and self-aware, with clarity about call and identity. Centering on a leader like Solomon provided a foundation for my confidence to grow. I became less frightened of disagreement, knowing that discourse and honest disagreement is part of living in a faith community.

Using the example of Solomon and his prayer request for leadership wisdom seems an important developmental task for any pastor. Claiming a leadership role and taking responsibility to purposefully lead the church is not for the timid of mind or spirit. For many years, I felt confined, like I was trying to wear leadership underwear two sizes too small. The more facilitative style of leadership just wasn't right for me. I would hasten to add that leadership styles, whether facilitative, directive, authoritarian, or some hybrid of these, do not alone make for an effective leader. There is no perfect way to lead; no model works in all situations, and no biblical term or symbol captures the diversity of congregational leadership demanded from pastors. The church needs pastors who have a passion for leading and guiding the church as well as the willingness and skill to adapt their leadership style to meet existing challenges.

In order to lead a congregation effectively, pastors count on lay leadership in the congregation to assist. When lay leadership responsibilities are abandoned, it puts both the congregation and pastor at risk. Likewise, when a pastor leads without seeking the wisdom of congregationally appointed leaders, it leaves the congregation vulnerable. Anabaptists and other faith traditions use a concept from 1 Pet 2:5, "the priesthood of all believers," to emphasize each member's important role. Of course, this theological concept functions best when the various parts of the body of Christ understand their unique gifts and responsibilities.

10

The Pastoral Review
—Refining Ministry

For by the grace given to me I say to everyone among you not to think
of yourself more highly than you ought to think, but to think with
sober judgment, each according to the measure of faith that God has
assigned.

—Rom 12:3

Journal Entry

My memo of understanding with the congregation calls for a pas-
toral review after three years. I am curious what this review will
turn up. I think the ministry is going well, but does the congrega-
tion have the same perceptions?

WORK LONG ENOUGH AT any job, and chances are there will be a
performance review of some kind. I had many of them as a public

school teacher. The building principal stopped by the classroom about once a quarter, without warning, to observe my teaching and classroom management. Later, he called me to his office to discuss his observations and provide feedback. Similarly, many denominations have a procedure for evaluating pastors, frequently referred to as "the pastoral review." However, important differences existed between my teaching evaluations and the pastoral reviews I encountered later.

The party doing the actual review was one major difference. In the congregation, all members were given the opportunity to share their points of view. In contrast, only one principal critiqued my teaching performance. I know of no other profession where all the stakeholders have this much influence. A second difference was related to authority. In the school, I knew who had ultimate authority: the principal. In the congregation, authority was diffuse, making it difficult to ascertain where true accountability resided. Was it in the formal structure of congregational leadership? Or did it reside in the informal network of congregational relationships?

Another major difference between the two processes was the clear set of expectations in the classroom versus the wide-ranging ones in the congregation. As a teacher, I knew the classroom behavioral protocols, including expectations for daily, weekly, and monthly lesson plans. In fact, when the principal walked into the classroom, I offered him my lesson plan book to demonstrate my diligence and commitment to using best practices as an educator. The same kind of specificity was missing for me as a pastor. Individual members had expectations, but those weren't necessarily the same as other members' notions of what I should be doing. Therein lay a significant challenge: clarifying group expectations.

Many congregations conduct pastoral reviews in haste, when a conflict is brewing, and without a clear job description on which to base the review. No wonder so many pastors dread them! Elimination of the pastoral review is not a solution, however. Performance reviews, when done well, can actually empower pastors, be a source of encouragement, and provide ideas for improvement. A pastor's divine call does not insulate her from the human frailties that beset church members. Pastors have the same motivations, limitations, and aspirations as congregants. Similarly, pastors evolve, change, become weary, and sometimes lose their ministry motivation. As a result, the pastor and the congregation do well to regularly review the pastor's performance as well as their ongoing relationship, similar to the early church's system of checks and balances for its leaders.

The conscientious Bible reader can discover examples in Scripture for negotiating the relationships between leaders and lay people. However much as we moderns would like to carve out a detailed pastor/congregational operational manual based on biblical instructions, it's not going to happen, because many specifics are missing. Yet we do find plenty of generalities and some very good ideas for considering people's relationship to their pastor. For instance, when the church at Jerusalem was growing rapidly, the new converts voiced expectations their leaders had not anticipated. Luke describes this new development and how the faith community responded: "Now during those days, when the disciples were increasing in number, the Hellenists complained against the Hebrews because their widows were being neglected in the daily distribution of food" (Acts 6:1). In response to these complaints, the church leaders changed how they related to the Hellenists. As a result, the faith community selected new leaders to assist in meeting the group's expectations. The message is clear: relationships between leaders and organizations frequently need re-contracting. What works at one development stage of the congregation might not work in another.

Likewise, 1 Cor 3:10 differentiates between one leader's gifts and those of another: "According to the grace of God given to me, like a skilled master builder I laid a foundation, and someone else is building on it. Each builder must choose with care how to build on it." In this passage, the Apostle Paul clarifies his role versus that of Apollo's. When the Corinthians wanted to take positions, one man over another, Apostle Paul deflected the tension by clarifying his own position. Paul said, "So I made up my mind not to make you another painful visit" (2 Cor 2:1). This verse serves as an introduction to an expanded dialogue in which Paul addresses the criticism directed toward him. Obviously, there were tensions between Apostle Paul and this congregation.

The post-Pentecostal churches also seemed relationally on edge, especially with their leaders. Little has changed, since the church is still fraught with relationship challenges. It's full of people who are both weak and strong. Some are fearful and demand answers to life's big questions; others are content to live with the questions, along with uncertainty and ambiguity. Some members are politically motivated and want more influence in the group. Many are quiet and desire nothing more than to live in harmony.

The stakes are high for congregations and pastors to work in tandem. Not tending the relationship will often lead to negative consequences. When I was a regional pastor, I catalogued twenty-two involuntary pastoral terminations during my fifteen-year tenure. All but a few of those twenty-two pastors chose not to continue in pastoral ministry and instead moved on to other professions. The point for sharing this data is to encourage congregations and their pastors to think strategically about their relationship because each deserves the best the other can offer.

Some parishioners will want to measure a pastor against a beloved former pastor. For example, not long ago I visited a pastor's office and commented on the oversized desk that took up much of the office space. The pastor, who was nearly dwarfed by this monstrosity, went on to respond that the desk was "immovable" because a cherished former pastor had donated it. He went on to say the former pastor even calls occasionally to ensure the desk is still being used. Long time members still comment on the generosity of the former pastor and recall the glory days of his leadership, during which time the church had grown considerably. In many respects, the current pastor was unintentionally being measured against his predecessor and the congregation that existed forty years ago.

Not all congregations have big desks that linger after a formative pastor leaves, but they will have memories that may or may not need revisiting. Both the incoming pastor and the congregation will build trust when they agree on the state of the congregation's current realities and opportunities for the future. Thinking strategically about congregational priorities and then carefully aligning them with the pastoral job description is not simply a current organizational fad; it is an absolute necessity! Congregations that do not clearly define what they are expecting from a pastor in light of their priorities leave open the possibility of missed opportunities. Conversely, pastors who do not assist their congregations in planning strategically for their current realities and future visions do them a disservice.

Many older congregations are experiencing declining attendance and smaller budgets. The results of this reality are ministry cutbacks, building neglect, and high membership anxiety. This stress often gets projected onto pastors, making the need for clear expectations and purposeful planning for the future even more important. If pastoral blame is left unchecked by lay leaders, these feelings escalate, and momentum grows for a pastoral transition.

Members also benefit when leaders provide them with standards of conduct and expectations for their behavior during conflict. If the Scriptures are somewhat vague on the specifics of pastor job descriptions, they are quite clear about congregational behavioral standards: "Welcome those who are weak in faith, but not for the purpose of quarreling over opinions" (Rom 14:1). First Corinthians 11:33 states, "So then, my brothers and sisters, when you come together to eat, wait for one another." Indeed, the Scriptures that speak to the expectations of believers seem endless, and yet controversy still prevailed. Do pastors need clear behavioral expectations? Yes, and most pastors I know are required to agree to sign some kind of a behavioral guideline before being ordained. Moreover, members need them as well, but rarely do pastors or lay leaders provide clear guidance, certainly missing an education and discipleship opportunity.

The pastor/congregation relationship is complex, and every pastor needs a few spiritually mature lay leaders surrounding her to add perspective and wisdom. For example, at the time of my first pastoral review, a committee was appointed to survey the congregation and ask members about their perception of my ministry. Obtaining congregational input seemed like a logical first step, but beyond that, I had no understanding or expertise in pastoral review protocols, nor did the lay leaders. When the survey was completed, the committee simply handed me a stack of completed forms, with no attempt to interpret or summarize the comments. I was looking at raw, unfiltered data. Of course, I read all of the comments with extreme interest, but one member's remark stood out like a stoplight on a freeway: "It is very difficult to listen to Larry's sermons when his child misbehaves during children's time." I read the sentence over and over in disbelief. I analyzed the handwriting. Who could have written this? The author must have been using 1 Tim 3:4–5 to form this pastoral critique. The Apostle Paul writes, "He [the bishop] must manage his own household well, keeping his children submissive and respectful in every way." This writer's appraisal of my three-year-old son and my implied lack of parenting skills became an obsession.

I re-created the incident over and over in my mind, trying to make sense of the incident he was referring to. I recalled the Sunday when my three-year-old son, tired from lack of sleep, had arrived at church hand in hand with his mother, looking as if he was in a cantankerous mood. As part of the worship routine, I led a brief children's time prior to the sermon. My grouchy son came forward and began squirming. He was probably thinking, "After all, this is my dad talking; I hear him talk all the time." I mistakenly tried to reprimand him in front of the church, and he responded with an "I hate you, Dad!" Those in attendance that day, at least the front rows, bore witness. My pastoral and parental ego took a big hit. Fortunately, the review committee graciously helped me put the negative response in perspective. They encouraged me to instead focus on the many positive comments—the gentle and caring advice I needed.

I had more pastoral reviews, and subsequent ones took on a greater sense of professionalism. For instance, the next review committee filtered all the comments and summarized them by topic. Rather than have me read what individuals wrote, they made a compilation similar to a picture collage. This necessitated that the committee spend more time with the reviews to discern what was being said. One of the biggest changes to the process was discussing the compiled pastoral review in my presence. In this face-to-face meeting, they were able to interpret the review for me, and I was able to ask questions of clarification. Inviting a regional judicatory or a trusted pastor peer to be part of this conversation would have been extremely beneficial as well, for it would have allowed another set of ears to help interpret the concerns and affirmations.

Congregational leaders and pastors can further enhance pastoral reviews by agreeing to a detailed pastoral job description—preferably prior to the pastor beginning ministry. However, it is never too late to create such a document. Job descriptions do not eliminate problems completely, but they go a long way toward putting limitations on member expectations. Compiling a job description may sound difficult, but it need not be a complex process.

Congregations are likely to elevate worship planning and preaching as pastoral priorities on a pastoral job description, particularly in smaller congregations. A wise congregation will clarify expectations related to these two areas of congregational ministry. Some specifics might include, but are not limited to:

- Preach four sermons per month.
- Conduct biannual training events for worship leaders, Scripture readers, communion assistants, and lay preachers.
- Include youth and children regularly in worship.
- Chair the worship committee and work collaboratively in planning for the congregation's worship needs.
- Consider membership diversity in planning sermons and worship.

Other areas of pastoral ministry—including education, pastoral care, community outreach, administration, and leadership—should each be similarly clear as to what is expected from the pastor.

All pastoral expectations need to relate directly to the congregation's broader vision. For example, if the congregation has a strong peace and justice emphasis as part of its vision in the community, the pastor's job description needs to reflect this priority. Here are a few statements that may greatly assist a pastor and congregation in clarifying expectations:

- Be visible in the community promoting the gospel of peace.

- Challenge the congregation with examples of justice and peace as taught by Jesus and reflected in all of Scripture.

- Create awareness within the congregation of global peace and justice concerns.

Clarifying expectations related to church administration is often dicey, especially in smaller and older congregations. In these congregations, lay leadership seems more deeply rooted and less open to sharing authority related to budget, building, and long-range planning—often for good reason. They have seen pastors come and go over the years, some with administrative abilities and some without. Giving management responsibility to pastors who lack knowledge and skill can do much organizational damage. In one rural congregation, the pastor and his family had so damaged the parsonage that it took months to repair and clean it after he left. This memory lasted through the next two pastors by severely limiting these pastors' ability to manage even their parsonage without first checking with the deacons. In another church, I discovered the pastor had full reign in planning worship but was required to ask the treasurer for a ream of paper. Why the distrust? The previous pastor had exceeded his office expenditures year after year. One pastor of an urban church lamented that the church's sign out front was outdated, could not be seen by passersby, and was useless for promoting weekly events. The change did happen—four years after the request went to the deacons. Why the delay? More research was needed, and the congregation had to be involved in the final decision.

Pastoral involvement in the congregation's budget and finances also needs clarity. Some pastors have input into the budget-setting process; many don't. Some pastors are included in capital campaigns, while others are not. Expectations need to be clear in order to prevent misunderstandings. For instance, during one church budget crisis, the pastor reported being excluded from the budget development stage even though the bylaws called for the pastor to be involved. Concerns were raised by the pastor, at the budget's size when it was presented to the congregation for approval. The congregation overlooked the pastor's concerns and passed the budget anyway. Then it became the pastor's job to cut the budget and carry the bad news to staff members who would need to take a salary reduction. Situations like this are stressful for the pastor and for the congregation, and it could have been prevented—or made less traumatic—had there been clarity in the pastor's administrative responsibilities related to budgeting.

One major advantage of having a detailed pastoral job description—apart from giving the pastor clarity—is to provide the congregation with a framework from which to review a pastor's ministry. A good review process will connect the pastoral survey directly to the job description. The review then becomes an educational tool that helps members understand the pastor's job in light of the congregation's expectations. A pastoral review also provides an opportunity for the pastor to self-reflect. The pastor can compare self-perceptions against others' views by completing the same survey. Hopefully, there will be no huge gaps between a pastor's view of her ministry and those of the congregation.

In an ideal situation, the pastoral review is never tied to the renewal of a contract. However, sadly, for some pastors, a congregational review becomes a referendum on pastoral tenure. In one congregation, the pastoral review results revealed stress between some members and the pastor. The committee overseeing the review was beginning to work on a strategy for addressing the issues, not anticipating what would happen next! A disgruntled group did the unexpected: they began contacting friends and other members to call for a pastoral vote, which was legal under the congregation's constitution. More than the usual number of people attended the congregational meeting, including many who had not been to church in a long time. Sadly, the pastor did not receive enough votes to stay and was forced to leave.

Similar stories, unfortunately, are all too numerous. Thus, leaders do well to keep job descriptions, constitutions, policy manuals, and bylaws—all these "dusty documents"—up to date. They serve as a road map and guide during difficult times. Second Kings 22:11 tells of King Josiah discovering the book of the law for the first time. The king's staff found the book while cleaning the temple. The passage reports the king "tore his clothes" as a sign of remorse at not knowing God's intentions. I use this story as a vivid illustration of the fallout that can occur when regular attention is not paid to a congregation's organizational documents. Keeping them relevant to current realities prevents unnecessary conflict, particular in times of formal pastoral reviews.

Between formal pastoral reviews, a less complicated and timely method of engaging specific members is to conduct mini-reviews. One practice I developed early in my ministry was asking members to provide feedback about my sermons. I handed out a mini-questionnaire to a few people ahead of worship time containing sermon-related questions. These informal reviews served a couple of functions: They helped me know if the sermon was connecting to congregants, and provided opportunities to be in conversation with members. More times than not, the person reviewing me would say, "Thank you for the opportunity." The mini-review leveled the hypothetical distance between pastor and layperson, demonstrating my vulnerability and openness.

As stated at the beginning of this chapter, a pastor is not above helpful critique. Well-planned pastoral reviews can assist with that assessment, as can informal methods of receiving feedback. These methods of building healthy relationships between pastors and parishioners go a long way toward solidifying and clarifying a pastoral call. After all, is there anything more critical to one's self-perception and sense of call than feeling appreciated? Congregations serve a momentous role in assisting their pastor to reinforce her calling from God. They do this best by providing a solid organizational structure that clearly defines the pastor/congregation relationship.

11

Routines, Leisure, Sabbaticals
—Nourishing Spiritual Growth

But he would withdraw to lonely places and pray.

—LUKE 5:16

Journal Entry

I didn't get my run in today, and I can tell because my attitude
sucks. Lord, thank you for the physical strength to exercise.
Thank you too for the energy and life I feel when this ritual is
consistent. Help me be patient when I fall short of meeting my
own expectations.

I SOMETIMES FORGET THE tentativeness and insecurity I felt during
the early years of pastoral ministry. The audacity of claiming the
authority to speak on behalf of God seemed almost overwhelming. The weight of the "pastor" title often felt heavy, like it might
be better carried by someone else. Yes, I went to seminary and

had previous work experience, but pastoral ministry was different from other vocations. I felt underprepared and over my head. I frequently asked God, "Are you sure about this calling? Maybe I'm just a phony?" I was young and immature.

I eventually learned, however, that my emotions of doubt, insecurity, and sense of being overwhelmed were passing and ever-changing, fickle and fleeting. They were not a good compass pointing toward a mistake in vocational direction. Rather, they were indicators that I needed to reclaim the whole of who I was apart from being a pastor. I needed to nurture the routines and interests that used to be life-giving—that provided emotional stability and perspective. Nurturing other dimension of my life built steadiness and continuity into the days, weeks, months, and years. They created balance and made the pastor role feel less stifling. My call stabilized and matured as I formed routines, prioritized leisure activities, and incorporated extended sabbatical leaves into my long-term planning. In contrast, when I was experiencing unrest during my public teaching career, the feeling stuck around like a pesky fly.

ROUTINES

I am a creature of habit and cannot understate the importance of routines. Those who are closest don't hesitate to point out my predictability. Not infrequently, one of my children will call and say, "Dad, let me guess what you're doing." Often their guesses are correct, not because they are fortunetellers, but because they know my habits.

Being routine-oriented sometimes gets a bad rap: "You're not spontaneous," people say, or "Routines don't allow room for the Holy Spirit," or "Routines are like a burial casket, only the two ends are missing." I've heard all these comments and more. But I take confidence in Jesus' propensity toward routine. The Gospels give indication that he too could be predictable. "He went to the synagogue on the sabbath day, as was his custom" (Luke 4:16b). "As was his custom, He taught them" (Mark 10:1). The Apostle Paul had his routines too: "And Paul went in, [the synagogue] as was his custom" (Acts 17:2). The phrase, "as was his custom," gives an indication that each had his routines.

Routines gave me life. Mondays and Saturdays were official days off, so I didn't go to the office. For the most part, I tried to respect these two days. Saturdays were free because sermons were finished by Friday, handwritten or typed up on the computer, word for word. Writing the sermon a few days ahead of Sunday gave it space to "ferment," to evolve for a day or so prior to Sunday. Once the sermon was written, I could relax and explore other ideas that might fit the theme. The completed sermon gave me freedom to venture beyond the written content, always looking for new ways to communicate the gospel.

Taking Saturdays off provided at least one weekend day dedicated to family. Because Sundays always found us at church, we seldom engaged in activities that involved the entire weekend. I remember an occasion when my nine-year-old son overheard some men making plans about going fishing the following weekend. Innocently, he asked if he and his dad could come too. What he heard was, "No, because your dad has to preach on Sunday." Whether the message was as direct as he remembers, what got interpreted was, "Your family is different from the rest of the congregation." In an attempt to minimize the impact of the pastoral role on my kids, I tried to keep Saturday as a non-church day, attending our children's soccer games or heading out of town for a day of fishing, hiking, or simply spending the day with them at home.

Early in ministry, I gained clarity that it would be best if I left the house before the rest of the family on Sunday morning. Otherwise, my pre-service anxiety telegraphed to the entire family, getting everyone off to an irritable start. As a result, I walked or rode my bike to church early to put the finishing touches on my sermon, pray, and prepare for worship.

Most weekday mornings, I tried to exercise with a jog or bike ride in the foothills near our home—sometimes with a friend, but often alone. Exercise provided uninterrupted time to pray and think about ministry, family, and current events. Many times, I was overcome with clarity of thought or brought to laughter or tears with a new insight. I always stopped to pray at some point in the exercise routine—often out loud—specifically naming my concerns, praises, and items of interest. Not infrequently, I knelt, raised my hands, or even lay down to express a physical connectedness to God. The nearly deserted foothills made my physical gestures feel less awkward. The freedom and oneness with God I felt using these unconventional prayer methods seem important.

On a balmy day during Lent, I spotted a great horned owl in a small wetland area. At the time of this particular owl spotting, I had been asking for God's guidance in making a big decision: Should I stay or should I go—as pastor to the congregation? This question of staying or going cycled throughout my fifteen-year tenure, often as a result of witnessing the implication of my work on my family. At this particular point in the cycle, the decision seemed particularly burdensome.

The owl sighting stopped me cold in my run. I stared at the owl in disbelief, and she stared back at me as my tears began to well up. Great horned owls are difficult to see, especially when not intentionally looking for one. They are night hunters but hang out in dead trees in the early mornings. At eighteen inches high, one might imagine them to be more obvious, but they are camouflaged to blend in with tree branches.

I interpreted this incident as a divine encounter. Of course, not everyone seeing the owl would have come to the same conclusion, but isn't the subjective nature of the religious experience all about interpretation? For instance, one person's experience with a bright light could be another's encounter with a great horned owl. Because of my chance meeting with the owl, the original question of whether to stay or leave the congregation shifted to the background as trust in God's leading guidance was reinforced. Of course, not all future owl sightings became lifelong faith-building experiences. However, in my heart and mind I am convinced God, via an owl, answered my prayer for reassurance. After this owl incident, my vocational questions and indecisions became irrelevant, at least for the time being. Not all routines lead to events that are as mystically significant as the one just described. However, when they do happen, they are a reminder that God is present even in life's everyday routines.

Keeping routines seems important, and one habit I developed early in ministry was keeping a time diary, tracking how many hours I worked and where my time was allocated. While punching a "time clock" is an unfamiliar routine for most, if not all, pastors, doing so might provide some surprising insights! How many hours a week are considered normal in a full-time pastorate? My denomination calculates a pastoral workweek at fifty hours. There is no doubt that pastors work hard and are only a phone call away from any member's crisis. Thus, a pastor's time is often difficult to manage. Pastors committed to the sanctity of routines and serving long-term need to be diligent at balancing parish demands with other aspects of life. Keeping a time diary is the beginning of leading a balanced life.

I generally arrived at the church office by eight in the morning. Most mornings were spent in the office as opposed to involvement in other ministries. Writing in my journal before there were interruptions was crucial. The journal allowed me the freedom to express emotions, thoughts, and concerns that might not otherwise find an outlet. The journal also gave me an opportunity to review the progress of a prayer concern over time. At the end of a month, a quarter, and a year, I would review my journal entries, asking specific questions. What topics occupied most of my writing energy? Where had God answered prayers? This chronology became a great tool for glimpsing the intersections of faith with activities of daily living.

Morning hours in the church office were not only for journal writing and praying, but also for reading the upcoming week's sermon texts. I read the Bible passages and then began to formulate a theme, trying always to apply and intersect the texts with congregational life as well as local and global current events. Mornings would also morph into administrative work and making phone calls. On Tuesday mornings, I would try to organize my week.

Planning the week ahead provided a valuable opportunity to manage time.

Most afternoons were set aside for community connections, pastoral visitation, and committee meetings. If I had evening commitments, I came home earlier in the afternoon to be with my family. I have never regretted the flexibility this vocation offered me. Yes, the routines guided my day, but they were easily adjusted around family needs too.

I share a few of these routines to illustrate how they gave my pastoral call stability and intention. When other professionals were punching a time clock, reporting to a manager, and measuring success via quarterly financial reports, I had a calling that was self-directed and unique. Routines provided me the structure from which to build a ministry and pastoral identity.

LEISURE

If routines bring stability to a pastor, then leisure time diverts attention from agendas, timetables, calendars, lists and plans, and meetings. Both are important. Cultivating leisure activities is critical to maintaining spiritual vitality because these non-pastoral pursuits give opportunity to change direction using a different set of gifts and interests. No pastor need be so singularly focused as to not play or follow a passion unrelated to their pastoral calling.

I'm not aware of a biblical text reporting that Jesus had a specific hobby or some recreational pastime, but a picture does emerge that portrays a life of some balance. And isn't balance really what the gift of leisure time is all about? According to the Gospel of Luke, "At daybreak he departed and went into a deserted place. And the people were looking for him" (Luke 4:42a). At the death of John the Baptist, Matthew writes, "Now when Jesus heard this, he withdrew from there in a boat to a deserted place by himself" (Matt 14:13a). From this extreme of Jesus being alone and separated from people, John's Gospel tells of Jesus socializing at a large wedding with his mother and disciples (John 2: 1–3). One of my favorite stories demonstrating Jesus' diversified interests is found in Mark 10:13–16: "Let the little children come to me; do not stop them; for it is to such as these the kingdom of God belongs" (Mark 10:14). The Gospels present a Messiah engaged in ministry, but also one involved in a variety of human endeavors, some pointing to self-care through privacy and relaxation.

Pastors I know spend leisure time collecting stamps, restoring cars, gardening, bicycling, knitting, reading, baking, or going to movies and plays. One pastor friend recorded Sunday's NASCAR race, then relaxed Sunday evening to watch it uninterrupted. His congregants knew not to tell him the race's outcome before he watched the delayed telecast. What one does to recharge and relax is not important. But a change of pace—a diversion—is important, just as it was for Jesus.

Having grown up in a working-class Midwestern family where manual labor was highly regarded, I assumed a man's identity was defined by his vocation. Calloused hands were evidence of a man who "knew the value of work." Leisure, for me, has had to be a learned behavior.

I soon found that relating to urban parishioners, especially in the Pacific Northwest, included learning to play. Congregational members, through example, taught me to enjoy and integrate recreation into my day-to-day life. As a result of their witness, I fell in love with bicycling, hiking, and cross-country skiing—along with the accompanying health benefits. These activities also provided conversation and common links with others in the congregation who prioritized recreation.

Pastors are caregivers, in a sense, and that role often results in giving to others at the expense of good self-care. Many pastors are out of shape physically, and not infrequently overweight too. Not only does excess weight shorten life expectancy, it also sends the wrong message to congregants: that the body isn't really God's temple. I readily acknowledge the demands of the profession that make it difficult to maintain regular exercise routines and keep good dietary habits. Members often want to provide the pastor a meal, and refusing is difficult, if not rude. When committee meetings happen at restaurants or members want us to join them for a meal, that also presents a challenge to eating healthily. Early morning or late night meetings do not allow for consistency in exercise routines either, but I still believe it is essential for pastors to engage in at least one activity that involves physical exertion. If more traditional forms of exercise are not an option, then discovering an activity that engages the body in some way is important—plus, it sets a positive example.

My wife and I purchased rental property many years ago that had cash flow potential. Often, the remodeling and renovation projects of fixer-uppers allowed me to work with my hands and use a growing tool collection. The properties also helped me feel empowered and self-sufficient, since I disliked being solely dependent on the congregation for financial security. The Apostle Paul's tent-making vocation provided a theological foundation to my interest in finding a way to earn a secondary source of income along with being a pastor: "And, because he [Paul] was of the same trade, he stayed with them [Aquila and Priscilla] and they worked together—by trade they were tentmakers" (Acts 18:3). Property repairs and maintenance were a form of leisure for me, since the projects provided a way to divert my attention and stay active.

Whether rental management, "tent-making," or some other vocation, a number of pastors I know cultivate a second source of income in their leisure time. For instance, one pastor contracted with a farmer to raise a few cows. This pastor wanted to be more self-sustaining and not leave his agricultural roots, even though he lived in the city. Friends and neighbors bought his meat when he butchered the animals. Another pastor turned a love for old classic books into a part-time vocation by buying and selling them for profit. One pastor bought undervalued cars and fixed them to resell. Another enjoyed crunching numbers. She started a bookkeeping business, and the business thrived. A hobby or special interest can be a great diversion to the demands of pastoral ministry. Hobbies turned into a source of income can also eliminate some of the budget pressure in smaller congregations where salary takes up a large percentage of the total budget.

SABBATICALS

Most denominations recommend that congregations grant pastors a periodic sabbatical leave. I took sabbaticals at years nine and thirteen of my pastorate. The sabbatical takes its origin from the biblical induction to leave the ground at rest after six years of tilling: "But in the seventh year there shall be a sabbath of complete rest for the land, a sabbath for the Lord: you shall not sow your field or prune your vineyard" (Lev 25:4). This farming illustration serves as the earliest biblical reference to best practices for land husbandry. Till the ground every year and the ground wears out; therefore, give the land a rest.

Many congregations are intentional in allowing their pastor time for rest and vocational recalibration, and other congregations need encouragement to do the same. While most vocations could benefit from sabbatical breaks in routine, the sabbatical tradition has unfortunately applied to only a few, with the church being only a recent benefactor.

My first sabbatical proved to be a cross-cultural experience for the whole family. I applied to a mission agency of our denomination for a one-year assignment and was fortunate enough to be accepted. While this agency normally took volunteers willing to commit for a minimum of three years, they granted permission for our family to volunteer in Jamaica for one year. In Kingston, Rebecca served as a nurse at a low-income clinic. My assignment was to visit denominational pastors to assess how our sponsoring agency could be of more assistance with their mission projects. Our children enrolled in local private schools.

This experience reshaped my ministry and gave our family an awakened awareness of the world. I returned with a new sense of purpose and commitment to my pastoral call. Working cross-culturally with eleven Jamaican pastors put my ministry back in the States in perspective. These pastors were passionate and thriving in their ministry despite much adversity, including poor economic conditions, lack of education, and few of the pastoral benefits afforded to their counterparts only an hour-and-forty-five-minute flight north across the Caribbean. They taught me to live with hope and expectancy even when surrounded by obstacles.

Our entire family benefited from this experience. Rebecca's time in Jamaica became the catalyst for a change in vocation. After returning home, she completed a degree in counseling. Our children became aware, for the first time, of their minority status. Their skin color was not the norm; they stood out in a crowd. They developed color blindness as they played soccer with mixed-race teams and attended school with Jamaican teachers. Both children talk fondly about this sabbatical year. Jamaica remains a special place for them, and the experience fostered a uniquely global perspective.

Meanwhile, back home, the local congregation enjoyed an interim pastor who was also taking a sabbatical and wanted to use his time in a completely new setting. Since my living expenses were paid in Jamaica by the sponsoring organization, my salary was used to pay the interim pastor. In fact, the interim pastor moved his family into our house for their sabbatical year. The congregation had grown up with me being their only pastor, but during this time away, they learned to appreciate another pastor and experienced both spiritual and numerical growth. Both the interim pastor and the congregation ranked the sabbatical experience as memorable and confidence-building. They learned to bond with a new leader, and I came back feeling relieved that I was not indispensible after all!

My second sabbatical was shorter—three months—and salaried. For one month, Rebecca and I stayed on San Juan Island, where we rented a cabin near the Puget Sound. By this time, we were officially empty nesters. We had a dream of writing a book about healthy marriage, so we wrote, prayed, watched the ferries come and go, and rode bicycles. The book was never accepted for publication, but we learned a lot about our marriage and ourselves.

During month two, we enrolled in Spanish language school in southern Spain, where we lived with a family and attended language school each day. Month three found us riding our bicycles across northern Spain on the Camino de Santiago to arrive at the famous Cathedral de Santiago on Good Friday.

This second sabbatical was altogether different from the first. The first was communal and the second solitary. I entered the second sabbatical asking God for a great horned owl of self-discovery. Surely, in a lonely house by the sea, in the isolation of a foreign country, or on a sacred Christian pilgrimage I would have clarity about my next steps in pastoral ministry. I did not find clarity, but I discovered something else—that God is present in the routine, everyday experiences of life, whether that is writing, sitting in a classroom learning Spanish, or riding a bicycle. The sabbatical provided the opportunity to discover once again what I had suspected: the sacred is everywhere. I just need to be present and aware enough to see the events around me and interpret the signs as they appear.

Sabbaticals provided a respite to the grinding pastoral pace. More specifically, my sabbaticals provided an opportunity to stand back and take a global view of life and ministry. The temporary leave also gave the congregation an opportunity to be self-sustaining. If before there had been pastoral dependence, that pattern was broken. New leaders stepped up, and new leadership allowed the congregation to witness another pastor and a different way of doing ministry.

12

Friendships
—A Life apart from the Congregation

Accordingly, though Jesus loved Martha and her sister and Lazarus,
after having heard that Lazarus was ill, he stayed two days longer in the
place where he was.

—JOHN: 11:5–6

Journal Entry

*I saw a cartoon that depicts the complexity of my church rela-
tionships. There were strings, lots of strings, all attached to the
bewildered looking pastor. The opposite end of each string connected to a church member. Strings were labeled with titles like:
budget committee chairperson, church council member, worship
participant, Sunday school teacher, pastor's friend, pastor's tennis
partner. The caption read, "Confused? Maybe you should be!" Is
it possible to be a pastor plus a congregant's intimate friend when
there are all these overlays? The verdict is still out!*

Friendships—A Life apart from the Congregation

EVEN THOUGH I WAS at the epicenter of many congregational gatherings and felt a tremendous amount of love and respect, I repeatedly felt alone. Despite my centrality to the life of the church and the close connections there, my relationships to parishioners seemed more one-sided than mutual. Conversations frequently focused on the congregation or on a specific challenge a member or his or her family was having. Although many congregants referred to me not only as their pastor, but also their friend, I felt confused at any given moment as to my role. Friendly conversations often became my pastoral work; after all, I was the pastor.

My inclination, especially early in ministry, was to try to fix whatever was bothering a member, especially if the problem related to congregational life. The perception that pastors were fixers kept me emotionally hooked and less able to be present when members shared. There were few issues I couldn't resolve, or so I thought. In one instance, two strong-willed committee members—co-chairs—were not getting along. I knew each woman as pastor and friend. Since both had confided in me about the challenges of working together, I decided to mediate between them. To this day, I regret my decision. I was not a "neutral," a precursor to being a good mediator. By inserting myself so directly in their relationship and trying to fix it, I became entangled, adding another layer to the already complicated roles I had in their lives—pastor, congregant, friend, and now mediator. In hindsight, I should have referred them to a neutral party with experience in managing conflict, but then again, pastors are often involved in complicated relationships.

Over time, and by taking advantage of continuing education opportunities like Clinical Pastoral Education and training to become certified as a mediator, I learned how to differentiate between my identity as a pastor and other parts of my life, including how to be a good friend, husband, and father separately and distinctly from being a pastor. What might seem easy hasn't been, and finding balance has become a lifelong learning assignment.

There is no better illustration of the subtleties between personal and pastoral relationships than the story of Jesus, Mary, Martha, and Lazarus. Chapter 11 of the Gospel of John provides a helpful glimpse into Jesus' identity as friend and companion over against his calling as shepherd and teacher. Jesus responded by raising Lazarus from the dead, but this miracle seems almost a sidebar news event. The headline that has always captured the imagination of readers is that Jesus wept with his friends. John 11:33–35 says: "When Jesus saw her [Mary] weeping, and the Jews who came with her also weeping, he was greatly disturbed in spirit and deeply moved. He said, 'Where have you laid him?' They said to him, 'Lord come and see.' Jesus began to weep." John's narrative about this incident describes Jesus as emotionally invested with friends. He feels their pain and responds with sympathy.

The same sympathy and compassion that we read in John chapter 11 isn't as noticeable when reading other gospel texts, however. Speaking to his mother at the wedding of Cana, Jesus says, "Woman, what concern is that to you and to me? My hour has not yet come" (John 2:4). Similarly, in his youth, Jesus disappeared, leaving his parents anxious. Jesus responds, "Why were you searching for me? Did you not know that I must be in my Father's house?" (Luke 2:49). While Jesus preached to crowds, someone pointed out that his mother and brothers were waiting outside to speak with him. The response Jesus gave to the person delivering the message seems to lack the expected empathy: "Who is my mother and who are my brothers?" (Matt 12:48).

Finding equilibrium between the healthy expression of intimacy on the one hand and wholesome boundary-setting on the other is an ongoing challenge for many pastors. Relationally intelligent pastors have the ability to experience intimacy with family, friends, and professional peers, and they also know how to maintain professional boundaries among their parishioners and in their work. Sadly, some will fall short of this goal.

A congregation should expect their pastor to be meaningfully connected in their denomination's leadership structure. Professional connections keep open a channel for dialogue among the stakeholders of a pastor's ordination credential. Likewise, a pastor needs to build relationships with congregational leaders. Together, they can discuss the pastor's time and ministry priorities.

Resistance to being accountable to leadership structures should be a warning sign. Such inaccessibility and emotional distancing is a seedbed for poor decision-making, especially as it relates to personal ethics, morals, and professional boundary violation. Remoteness and isolation seem to breed a seductive sense of power, and power is ultimately only an illusion.

Matthew 12:43–45 describes an empty house that is swept clean only to be invaded by demonic spirits. Pastors with an empty house—a vocation without a sense of community or connectedness—run the risk of losing their moral check-and-balance system. One friend and pastoral peer suffered a moral failure when he had inappropriate sexual activity with a parishioner. I was shocked! How does this happen? How can a pastor justify a break in pastoral trust of this severity? The negative consequences to his family and congregation would seem to outweigh any momentary pleasure from indiscretion, but unfortunately rational thought is seldom at the forefront during boundary violations.

Leaders, including pastors, strengthen their personal identity and their vocational call when they define appropriate limits. For instance, I strive to have intimacy with my immediate family because I want them to know I am a husband and father first. Of course, discussing matters of faith with them is important, but I am clear about not being their pastor. The same approach would apply to a few good friends: I am first a friend, not their pastor. The role only changes at their request. Likewise, I am called to be the best pastor possible by being fully present with congregants and sharing appropriately, but mostly listening. Though I can be a friend and experience a level of intimacy with some members, my primary calling is to be a pastor to the community. I also have meaningful relationships with professional peers, apart from the congregation. Finally, I have professional relationships with my conference minister as well as with a spiritual friend or director. Not unlike the marriage bond, the pastoral call, as acknowledged by the ordination credential, is held in trust with all these varied relationships.

This community of varied relationships didn't happen quickly, however. It evolved over time, with four relationship categories emerging: family, friends, pastor peers, and structured formal relationships. There was some overlap between the groups, but each served a vital function.

FAMILY

Community began at home. I am married, so that relationship came first. Prioritizing this relationship was critical if I was going to have personal and professional integrity. Apart from pastoral ministry, marriage was my life-blood, a crucial aspect of my personal identity as a man and a husband. Rebecca was a spiritual confidant and my closest friend. We regularly talked about my pastoral work. I relied heavily on her insights, both as a woman and as a spiritual peer. She was truly a partner, especially in the early days of church planting, but also throughout my ministry. I've heard other pastors tell me they don't talk much to their spouses about church work. My pastoral ministry would not have been successful without Rebecca's support and commitment to our family, her faith, and me.

Our children did the most to ground my pastoral call in the reality of every day life. They never allowed my pastor title to stand in the way of honest conversation or their own lifestyle choices. The friends they brought into my life greatly enriched my understanding of a different generation. One of our son's friends felt enough kinship to call us "Ma" and "Pa." Our daughter's friend lived with us through some troubled times, and to this day she considers us a second set of parents. Their adolescence was not particularly easy for me, but it now seems like a distant memory. Both children have grown up to be wonderful, caring, faith-filled, and compassionate adults, and they have now given their mother and me wonderful sons- and daughters-in-law and grandchildren. I can say, without hesitation, that pastor's kids have a unique calling that few will ever fully grasp, unless of course they are one.

Two other family members, now deceased, had a significant function in my pastoral community: My mother and my father-in-law. Vince was a "church junkie." He loved the church and loved talking about the church. He worked in church institutions all of his professional life and was familiar with church structures and politics. He was a stabilizing force early in ministry. If I wanted a voice of reason and wisdom, I would call Vince.

My mother, in contrast to Vince, was not a person wise to the ways of the organized church, but she had commonsensical wisdom about people that cut to the quick of issues. For instance, during one of our weekly Sunday evening phone calls, I shared a concern that a family was threatening to leave the congregation. "Why would they do that?" she asked.

Hesitantly, not knowing how she might respond, I replied, "Because two gay women attending the church are living together."

Without missing a beat, she replied rather curtly, "People just need to mind their own business." She transitioned just as quickly to telling me about the wonderful rain and beautiful green beans she had just picked. Hearing my eighty-year-old mother, who grew up in a small Midwestern congregation deeply embedded in her lifelong Christian faith, so succinctly contextualize my concern felt extremely freeing. I took a deep breath and smiled.

FRIENDS

I was fortunate to have good friends outside the congregation. These friends were important because they kept me engaged in the language of the world apart from the church. When I leaned toward the serious, mysterious, heavy, or burdensome aspects of the pastoral vocation in our conversations, my friends might say, "Hauder, you need to lighten up. Hey, did you hear the one about the man who asked the Rabbi if having sex on the Sabbath was work or play?" For these friends, religion was a tradition, a set of beliefs, not a vocation as it was for me, and when I took life too seriously, they reminded me with a smile that maybe I needed to "get a real job."

A friend from high school and I have stayed closely connected over the years, even though we live eight hundred miles apart. Phone conversations reminiscing our high school days, a quick text message referencing a good book, an email related to an upcoming travel itinerary, and occasional photos of our bread-making endeavors have provided me a grounding in reality. He knows where I came from, and we share a common small-town legacy.

A neighbor also became a close friend, primarily because we had children the same age. As a Jew who was heavily involved in the local synagogue, he occasionally invited our family to the Seder services his family planned. When his children reached adolescence, we were invited to each of their bar and bat mitzvah services. We discovered common values of family, faith, and tradition in those more formal times and in our early morning bike ride conversations.

A former Baptist turned Quaker turned community organizer became a friend after he and his family briefly attended the congregation where I was pastor. We jogged together and told stories of growing up in small Midwest towns and tiny evangelical congregations. It was this friend who made a startling request one day while running: "Since I can't lie to you, will you ask me on occasion if I'm keeping integrity with my marriage vows? This will help keep me honest."

I sold a rental property two doors down to a stranger who soon became my friend as well as my neighbor. We were quite the odd couple, for his worldview had no place in it for God, and, as far as I know, he was never attracted to any religion. This relationship evolved through hour-long coffee break conversations, sharing tools, and my requests for help with home repair projects. His view of the world was so different from mine, yet our friendship matured. We agreed, informally, not to talk about our differences. I learned that spirituality is much broader than a statement of belief. Imagine the surprise when he was suddenly diagnosed with inoperable stage-four cancer and given eighteen months to live. He appointed me as his estate's administrator. His legacy continued as he redefined my understanding of generosity and began giving away his substantial estate to organizations that were ministering to women and children in need.

The following experience with two friends seems important to retell, for it gives a flavor of quality friendships, intimacy, and good boundaries: In late October of every year, after the sugar beets had been trucked to the factory, two friends—one a farmer, the other another pastor—and I traveled four hours to the Jarbidge River Canyon. We sat three abreast—with me, the youngest, in the middle—in a four-wheel drive, fifteen-year-old F-250 Ford pickup. On arrival, we set up a hunter camp, even though none of us were serious hunters. The tent was big enough for a table, chairs, propane stove, and three army cots. Each morning after a late breakfast, we fished, hunted chukar, and searched for the occasional rare geode, but mostly we talked, laughed, and ate hearty meals cooked in cast-iron skillets. We had one communication rule: Anything said on this trip could not be repeated, even with a spouse, unless there was a common agreement.

During the late afternoon hours, as the sun disappeared over the canyon wall, the three of us took turns walking to the makeshift bathtub earlier visitors had rigged up. After adjusting the old galvanized pipe that fed the hot water into the tub, I soaked in the natural spring water while I stared out across the desolate, treeless, boulder-strewn canyon, complete with a ribbon of water flowing into the Jarbridge River. This trip was a detour, a life-giving diversion—one I looked forward to each fall. The isolation and intimacy combined to make these trips restorative to my soul long after the trip was over.

PROFESSIONAL PEERS

Pastor friends were important because they provided a forum for speaking professionally. We shared common vocations and a commitment to pastoral excellence. These peer connections provided a place to "talk shop," to confess, to laugh, to mourn, and to pray for one another's ministry. Dialogue between us might go like this: "I had the craziest thing happen last Sunday. A visiting couple cornered me before the service and asked if I preach the Bible, because their last pastor didn't. How would you respond?" One pastor, ten years my senior, usually had the quickest retort: "Tell the visitor to stick around and see for himself. But if your former pastor didn't preach the Bible, I doubt you'll think I do either!" Bob was the same pastor peer who stopped a divisive unsigned letter from gaining momentum at a large assembly of congregations. He brought a paper shredder to the pulpit area and proclaimed that the church is about speaking openly, one to another.

My ecumenical friends helped me learn the language of ecumenism. I was often a guest speaker at their congregations, where I discovered we had many similarities. I belonged to a Bible study group that met at our church and was made up of three Episcopalians, two members of the Church of the Brethren, two Quakers, and two Mennonites. A retired Episcopalian priest and I cultivated a close friendship apart from the group that lasted until his death. I asked him the questions I was unable to ask others. We were ecumenical peers—he was an older and wiser and not my denominational pastor.

Conversations with pastor peers had no power differential, and because of this neutrality, we could share issues concerning our congregations without fear of repercussion. We had a safe place to talk without severely implicating our jobs. As a result, I found these relationships profoundly important. These pastors gave equilibrium to my pastoral call and helped me keep perspective.

STRUCTURAL RELATIONSHIPS

Structural relationships—connections that are created because of job title and organizational polity—are important too. In my denominational hierarchy, the conference minister had pastoral oversight responsibilities for pastors in the conference. The conference minister role was frequently described as a "pastor to the pastors." I was fortunate enough to have the same conference minister for my entire first pastorate. He was a person grounded in good process versus the use of authority. He invited dialogue rather than provided answers. He remained a mentor and confidant years later after I assumed his role as conference minister.

Many pastors invite and even pursue the spiritual oversight their judicatories often provide, but some don't. As stated earlier, this avoidance is a danger sign for the pastor and the congregation. Without pastoral oversight both within and outside the congregation, pastors can make poor choices. When I became a judicatory, I found it painless and easy to cultivate a meaningful relationship with some pastors, but it was difficult and complicated with others who seemed to want little accountability or connectivity to the district or denomination. Congregations do well to encourage, even demand, that their pastor foster a relationship with a bishop, conference minister, district pastor, or a judicatory—whatever title.

Additional options for oversight and accountability include mental health therapists and spiritual directors. Any relationship, apart from the congregation, that is both intentional and professional and is created for the purpose of honest reflection about ministry can be effective at keeping integrity in the pastoral call. I've mentioned the relationship with my conference minister, but I had other professional relationships as well. I sought out a former Nazarene pastor who was also a psychologist in private practice. His pastoral and psychological insights were invaluable. I paid for his services out of my personal funds for over a year, and I found the expense worthwhile and the conversations invaluable. He provided needed ministry perspective and challenged my thinking, if necessary.

During one phase, I tried designating my former Catholic priest friend as a spiritual director, but the role never quite worked for him or for me. Later, I met with another friend, the ex-Baptist, to pray, read Scriptures, and to "hold each other accountable." That relationship worked for a short time, but the formality eventually petered out, leaving us with the friendship, but not the spiritual intentionality. These experiments led me to conclude that intentional relationships for the purpose of spiritual accountability need external reinforcement—at least they did for me. When I paid for counseling services, arriving on a scheduled time and date, the meeting became a priority. Likewise, when I was expected to have a relationship with my conference minister in order to keep my ordination credential in good standing, I gladly made that relationship a priority.

Being a responsible and effective pastor required a community effort. Without friends, colleagues, and family, my ministry would have been short-lived and lacking in either passion or intensity. I have become more cognizant, with some distance from active ministry, of how all of these connections served to strengthen my pastoral call. No longer was it only my call; it belonged to many people because they all shared the joys and challenges surrounding it.

Conclusion

HOPEFULLY, A PASSION FOR pastoral ministry and a renewed vision for the local congregation have taken root after reading *Called to Be a Pastor*. As stated in the introduction, a strong and healthy relationship between congregations and their pastors is crucial if either one is to live up to their high calling. The Apostle Paul writes powerfully in Eph 2:19–22 about the role of the church—this human institution infused with a divine purpose. He refers to it as the "holy temple" and a "dwelling place for God" (Eph 2:19–22). The local congregation serves as the catalyst for implementing this New Testament vision of church.

When the norms of society promote divisiveness and a fear of individual differences, the local church's welcoming voice needs to be heard. When saber rattling across the world grows more intense, Jesus' message of peace needs proclamation. When economic inequities make hope more difficult, the New Testament's example of community and church needs to be revisited. The church's mission has never been more important! Congregations function at their highest potential in fulfilling this mission when their pastors are driven by conviction, empowered by a sense of divine call, informed by practical leadership skills, and in love with the people they serve.

A final word of encouragement is important for the seeker still working at a day job but speculating whether God may be calling her or him into professional pastoral ministry. If you feel restlessness about your current vocational pursuit, as I was, surround yourself with wise and deliberate people who know you and understand your situation. There is no substitute for time and testing. And then, ultimately, you will take the responsibility for addressing the impatient yearnings you feel. May Moses' words of encouragement to Joshua be yours: "Be strong and bold; have no fear or dread of them, because it is the Lord your God who goes with you; he will not fail you or forsake you" (Deut 31:6).

Lightning Source UK Ltd.
Milton Keynes UK
UKOW06f1549300816

281805UK00001B/63/P